Johannesburg, South Africa

Travel and Tourism Guide

Author
Caleb Gray.

SONITTEC PUBLISHING. All rights reserved. No part of this publication may be reproduced, distributed, or transmitted in any form or by any means, including photocopying, recording, or other electronic or mechanical methods, without the prior written permission of the publisher, except in the case of brief quotations embodied in critical reviews and certain other noncommercial uses permitted by copyright law. For permission requests, write to the publisher, addressed "Attention: Permissions Coordinator," at the address below.

Copyright © 2019 Sonittec Publishing
All Rights Reserved

First Printed: 2019.

Publisher:
SONITTEC LTD
College House, 2nd Floor
17 King Edwards Road,
Ruislip
London
HA4 7AE

Table of Content

SUMMARY 1
INTRODUCTION 6
   PHYSICAL AND HUMAN GEOGRAPHY 7
      The landscape 7
         The city site 7
         Climate 9
         The city layout 10
THE PEOPLE 15
THE ECONOMY 17
   COMMERCE AND INDUSTRY 17
   TRANSPORTATION 18
ADMINISTRATION AND SOCIAL CONDITIONS 20
   GOVERNMENT 20
   PUBLIC SERVICES 21
   HEALTH 22
   EDUCATION 23
CULTURAL LIFE 25
HISTORY 28
   THE EARLY PERIOD, 1853–1930 28
      Boomtown 28
      Consolidation of the gold industry 31
      The national and international context 33
      The local level 36
      Challenge by white workers 39
   THE TRANSFORMATIONS OF THE 1930S AND '40S 40
   APARTHEID 43
      Enforcing the system 43
      Apartheid's demise 45
TOURISM 48
   GUIDE TO JOHANNESBURG 49
   FAMILY TRIP WITH KIDS 54
   CUISINE & RESTAURANTS 58
      Tashas, between cafe and fine dining 61

    Perron, Johannesburg's Mexican touch 63
    A truly unique brunch at Salvation Café 64
    Turn 'n Tender: real meat from a real family 66
    The Butcher Shop and Grill 68
    Sakhumzi 69
    Moyo: the place for hip gourmets 71
    Kitchener's Carvery Bar 72
    44 Stanley 74
TRADITIONS & LIFESTYLE 76
CULTURE: SIGHTS TO VISIT 79
ATTRACTIONS & NIGHTLIFE 82
ART CULTURAL SIGHTS 85
    Afrikaner heritage and a newly named urban area 85
    Zulu art 87
    Cradle of Humankind: a remarkable paleontological site 88
    Soweto: victory against apartheid 90
    Museum Africa: national history on display 92
    Goodman Gallery 93
    From Constitution Hill to Carlton Centre 95
    David Krut Projects: front-row culture 96
TIPS FOR TOURISTS 98
SHOPPING IN JOHANNESBURG... 101
WHY JOHANNESBURG IS BECOMING AFRICA'S HIPPEST CITY 106
GOING TO JOHANNESBURG FOR THE FIRST TIME 127
THINGS TO KNOW AHEAD OFGOING TO JOHANNESBURG 136
JOHANNESBURG DIVERSITY SHAPING ENVIRONMENT AND LIFESTYLE .. 151
INDISPENSABLE PLACES TO VISIT IN JOHANNESBURG 168

Johannesburg, South Africa

Summary

The importance of travelling in our life?
Everyone has their very own reasons to travel. Some people travel for work, some travel for pleasure while for others it is just a way of life. They travel to live and to escape at the same time.

Whatever might be the reason to travel, here are few ways in which travelling would definitely change you and I think that is why travelling becomes so important in life:

<u>Enjoy being alone</u>: There is something therapeutic about being alone and being at peace with it.

While you soak in a new culture, you also connect with your own inner self.

Learn to adapt: It is a different world out there, literally. Be it the pace of life, the language or simply the change in weather, it is always a change and you have to adapt to it. This is what makes travelling truly beautiful as you break away from the routine and adapt to something totally new.

Experience a new culture: Every place comes with its distinct cultural habits, you cannot think about New York without talking about its fast paced life and about Italy without enjoying its relaxed lifestyle. Similarly, while visiting the UK you might have to be a bit formal in your interactions with the locals, on the other hand, while greeting the people in Thailand, one can be really warm and casual.

Johannesburg, South Africa

<u>Broaden your taste buds</u>: Travelling without experiencing the local food is just not complete. It is not only a culinary experience but a cultural one as well.

<u>Get out of comfort zone</u>: From simple experiences like the weather, way of life or food to the more adventurous ones like trying a new sport, travelling really pushes ones boundaries to the core. You might end up participating in a street carnival in Brazil just like the locals or trying the local delicacies (read insects) in Thailand.

<u>Indulge in Photography</u>: It does not matter whether you are a professional or not. It is also irrelevant whether you have a DSLR or a very basic camera, while travelling what matters is the love and quest for seeing beautiful places and the sheer joy of capturing them in your lense. Travelling would in return give you your very own collection

of amazing postcards of beautiful sunsets, snow laced mountains or sunny beaches.

Learn to escape: Travelling is the best way to break the routine. If you are in a bustling city, go ahead and experience the country life. If you are in a rural place, travel to a bustling city and experience its madness. Stressed with the city life or work pressure? A spa break in Himalayas or Kerala is a must try.

Appreciate Nature: The quest to explore more when one is travelling always leads to a sense of amazement about nature. While most of us keep a track of technological advancements, Nature has its own ways of outshining all of these. The Antelope Canyon in Arizona or Turquoise Ice in Russia are the finest examples of this. For more, check out the most unbelievable places around the world.

Johannesburg, South Africa

<u>Get closer to your own roots</u>: While one travels and experiences a lot of different cultures and practices, it definitely brings one closer to his or her own roots. Travel helps one appreciate one's identity and culture.

Travelling is all about experiences. They can happen in terms of culture, people, places but most importantly with one's own self and this was all about

Introduction

Johannesburg, city, Gauteng province, South Africa. It is the country's chief industrial and financial metropolis.

One of the youngest of the world's major cities, Johannesburg was founded in 1886, following the discovery of gold. The city was initially part of the Transvaal, an independent Afrikaner, or Boer, republic that later became one of the four provinces of South Africa. Today the city is a part of Gauteng (a Sotho word meaning "Place of Gold"), one of the nine provinces of South Africa.

Johannesburg, South Africa

The geography of Johannesburg reflects nearly a century of racially driven social engineering that reached a climax under apartheid (literally "apartness"), the system of racial segregation that obtained in South Africa from 1948 to 1994. The result is a city of extraordinary contrasts, of glass and steel skyscrapers and fetid shantytowns, of internationally recognized universities and widespread illiteracy, of glittering abundance and desperate poverty. Pop. (2005 est.) urban agglom., 3,288,000.

Physical and Human Geography

The landscape
The city site

Johannesburg is situated on the Highveld (*see* veld), the broad, grassy plateau that sweeps across the South African interior. The city bestrides the Witwatersrand, or Rand, a string of low, rocky ridges that constitutes the watershed between the drainages into the Indian and Atlantic oceans. The city's elevation ranges from 5,700 to 5,930 feet (1,740 to 1,810 metres).

Aside from a few small streams and artificial lakes, Johannesburg lacks water. The city owes its location to the presence of an even more precious resource: gold. The city grew on the edge of the Witwatersrand Main Reef, a subterranean stratum of gold-bearing quartz-silica conglomerate that arcs for hundreds of miles beneath the Highveld. Most of the gold mines in the city ceased operation in the 1970s, but in its day the Witwatersrand gold industry accounted for more than 40 percent of the world's annual gold production. Remnants of the industry rusting headgear, towering yellow-white mine dumps, copses of dusty Australian bluegum trees imported for underground timbering still litter the landscape.

Climate

Johannesburg has a temperate climate. Summertime temperatures average about 75 °F (24 °C); winter temperatures average about 55 °F (13 °C) and only occasionally dip below freezing. The city enjoys about eight hours of sunlight per day in both winter and summer. Rainfall averages about 28 inches (700 millimetres) per annum, but the total varies considerably from year to year. Droughts are common. What rain the city receives falls almost exclusively in the summer months, often in spectacular late-afternoon electrical storms. Air pollution poses a significant problem, especially in the winter months, when thermal inversions impede the westward flow of air from the Indian Ocean. Pollution is most severe in the densely settled black townships on the city's periphery, where many residents still rely on coal for fuel.

The city layout

Central Johannesburg, the commercial and financial heart of South Africa, is laid out in a rectangular grid pattern that is unchanged from the first city survey in 1886. Streets are narrow and cast into shadow by high-rise concrete blocks, creating an almost tunnellike effect. Architecturally, the city is a hodgepodge, reflecting decades of rapid growth and a singular indifference to historic preservation. The tents and clay huts of the original mining camp are gone, as are most of the ornate, gabled Victorian edifices that sprang up in the 1890s. (Markhams Building, on Pritchard Street, is a conspicuous exception.) The early 20th century brought a variety of architectural styles and movements. Monumental Beaux Arts structures such as the Supreme Court building and the Johannesburg Art Gallery bespoke the city's new status as an outpost of the British Empire, while massive, steel-reinforced concrete blocks such as Corner House, headquarters of one of South Africa's leading mining houses, reflected the growing importance of American architectural techniques and idioms. American influence was even more apparent in the 1930s "skyscraper" movement, most notably in the 1937 ESKOM Building, a 21-story Art Deco tower built to evoke the vigour of New York City. (The ESKOM Building was torn down in 1983, joining a distinguished line of vanished landmarks.) Whatever architectural distinction the city had was lost in the decades after World War II amidst a sea of nondescript high-rise blocks.

Greater Johannesburg, an area of more than 200 square miles, comprises more than 500 suburbs and townships. Under the terms of the 1950 Group Areas Act, the cornerstone of urban apartheid (see below), each was reserved for a single "race group." The act was repealed in 1991, but Johannesburg retains a high degree of racial segregation.

Black Africans can be found throughout the city, but the majority still live in "townships" on the urban periphery, essentially dormitory cities for blacks working in the city. Alexandra township, a 20-square-block enclave carved out of Johannesburg's white northern suburbs, houses a population of nearly half a million. At least three times that number live in Soweto (South-West Townships), a sprawling urban complex 10 miles southwest of the city. Johannesburg's small Coloured population (people of mixed race) clusters in townships west of the city, while the bulk of its Indian population (ethnic Asians: Indians, Malays, Filipinos, and Chinese) lives in Lenasia, a special "Asiatic" township built in the 1950s to accommodate Indians forcibly removed from the city centre. The balance of the city is occupied by whites.

Accommodation varies in character and quality. Soweto is notorious for its endless rows of municipally built, two-room matchbox homes, yet it also has a few prosperous enclaves as well as teeming squatter camps, where tens of thousands live without water, electricity, or sanitation facilities. Black migrant workers, long the backbone of South Africa's industrial labour force, are lodged in massive, single-sex hostels located close to the workplace or on the edge of black townships. White accommodation varies from suburb to suburb. In western suburbs such as

Brixton and Melville, middle-class whites live in the modest tin-roofed bungalows and semidetached homes that once housed the city's white working class. Conditions are bleaker in neighbouring suburbs such as Cottesloe, Vrededorp, and Booysens Reserve, home to most of Johannesburg's white poor. More affluent whites live in the north, in leafy, established communities such as Houghton and Parktown, once the residence of South Africa's mining magnates, or in any of a dozen newer suburbs. Northern suburban homes typically include large, flowering gardens and swimming pools. Most are surrounded by high fences.

The people

About three-fourths of Johannesburg's citizens are black, fewer than one-fifth are white, and most of the remainder are Coloured or Asian/Indian. Such figures, however, scarcely do justice to the city's polyglot population. At least a dozen different languages are in widespread daily use in Johannesburg. The majority of the white population is of English and Afrikaans descent, but the city also includes substantial Portuguese, Greek, Italian, Russian, Polish, and Lebanese communities. The black population includes representatives from every ethnic and linguistic group in southern Africa. All the world's major religions are represented, though the majority of the people, both white and black, are Christian. The most significant churches, in terms of numbers, are the "Zionist" churches small, independent African sects that blend Pentecostal Christianity and indigenous ritual belief. Zionists, adorned in colourful robes, hold outdoor services all across the city on Sundays.

The economy

Commerce and industry

Johannesburg is a centre of mining, manufacturing, and finance. All the mining houses are headquartered in the city, as is the Chamber of Mines, which regulates the industry. Local factories in Johannesburg and on the East Rand produce a great variety of goods ranging from textiles to specialty steels. A substantial engineering sector serves the needs of the mining industry. Virtually all the country's banks, insurance companies, and building societies have their head offices in the city. The Johannesburg Stock Exchange, founded in 1887 to raise capital for deep-level mining, lists more than 600 companies.

While Pretoria, the South African capital, is only 40 miles to the north, most state ministries have offices in Johannesburg. Many foreign countries retain consular facilities, largely to service the needs of overseas firms, hundreds of which operate in the city.

Transportation

Johannesburg is a hub for local, national, and international travel. Railroads and multilane freeways crisscross the metropolitan area, carrying hundreds of thousands of daily commuters to and from outlying suburbs and townships. South Africa's first high-speed train, the Gautrain, links Johannesburg with Pretoria as well as stops along the way; another spur connects with nearby O.R. Tambo International Airport. A municipal bus system operates within the city, and a separate, private bus company operating under a state monopoly connects the city centre with Soweto and Alexandra. The inadequacies of the latter have fostered a burgeoning local taxi industry. O.R. Tambo International Airport, 14 miles northeast of the city centre, offers regularly scheduled service between Johannesburg and most cities in southern Africa, as well as direct flights to Europe, North and South America, Australia, and Asia.

Administration and social conditions

Government

South Africa possesses a federal system of government, with authority divided between national, provincial, and local levels of government. Local authority for Johannesburg rests with the City of Johannesburg Metropolitan Municipality, which includes representatives from all across the metropolitan area. In extending the municipal borders to include previously disfranchised black townships such as Soweto and Alexandra, political leaders hope to facilitate some equalization of revenues and services between white and black areas.

Public services

Local bus service, fire fighting, and sanitation remain the province of the municipality, but other responsibilities such as the provision of housing in black townships have been assumed by the Gauteng regional legislature. Most electricity is provided through the Electricity Supply Commission (ESKOM), a national parastatal institution; privately owned power stations also provide some electricity to the city. Water is supplied by the Rand Water Board. Municipal police oversee traffic control; other policing is provided by the South African Police Services. The South African Broadcasting Corporation is headquartered in Auckland Park, west of the city centre.

Health

Apartheid left perhaps its deepest imprint on public health. In black townships rates of child mortality are significantly higher and life spans far shorter than in white neighbourhoods. Tuberculosis, virtually eradicated among whites, remains endemic in townships and migrant hostels. Addressing such historical inequities is one of the chief challenges of the national government.

Johannesburg has numerous hospitals and clinics, designated under apartheid for use by specified race groups but now legally open to all. The best-equipped of these is Johannesburg General, a 2,000-bed formerly "white" hospital that opened on Parktown Ridge in 1978. The largest hospital in Johannesburg, and indeed in all Africa, is Baragwanath, a sprawling complex on the northern edge of Soweto; it serves more than

5,000 patients per day, placing a severe burden on limited facilities. With the end of segregation, an increasing number of whites have resorted to expensive "private clinics," where they receive treatment equivalent to that in a modern American hospital.

Education

Primary and secondary schools range widely in character. Racial segregation, abolished in law, remains common in practice. Facilities of higher education include the University of the Witwatersrand, South Africa's premier university. Founded in 1896 as the South African School of Mines, "Wits" today confers degrees in commerce, arts, sciences, architecture, law, education, medicine, and dentistry. Also there is the University of Johannesburg, formed in 2005 when Rand Afrikaans University, Technikon

Witwatersrand, and local campuses of Vista University merged.

Johannesburg, South Africa

Cultural life

Johannesburg boasts a rich, if strangely schizophrenic, cultural life. Patrons of the arts can take in a performance of the National Symphony Orchestra and then retire to one of the city's thriving jazz clubs to hear internationally acclaimed local performers, many of whom have returned to Johannesburg after long years in exile. The Johannesburg Art Gallery, established in the early years of the 20th century with donations from mining magnates, features Africa's finest collection of European Impressionists, while most of the city's dozen private galleries increasingly highlight the work of African artists. Theatre flourishes.

While the 1,100-seat Civic Theatre stages European operas and American musicals, many smaller companies nurture the talents of local actors and playwrights, white and black. A visit to Johannesburg is incomplete without a trip to the world-renowned Market Theatre, a multitheatre complex housed in the city's old produce market.

The city has many museums and libraries. Johannesburg Public Library, first established in 1889, is the centre of an extensive network of branch libraries. Local museums specialize in geology, Africana, military history, archaeology, transport, banking, costume, and Judaica. Visitors interested in a taste of old Johannesburg can visit Gold Reef City, an amusement park located a few miles south of the city on the site of a defunct gold mine. Those interested in a less-sanitized version of the city's past can visit the nearby Apartheid Museum. Museum Africa and the Bensusan

Museum of Photography are both at the old market.

Blessed as they are with a warm sunny climate, Johannesburgers spend a considerable amount of time outdoors. The northern suburbs feature broad swaths of open space for bird-watching and picnicking. Weekend cookouts *braaivleis*, in local parlance are a summertime ritual, especially among Afrikaners. Like other South Africans, Johannesburg residents tend to be avid sportsmen. In the years since South Africa's return from political isolation, the city has hosted international competitions in rugby, football (soccer), cricket, golf, and tennis.

History
The early period, 1853–1930
Boomtown

Johannesburg's early history is the story of gold. In 1853 Pieter Jacob Marais, a South African prospector, recovered alluvial gold from the Jukskei River, north of what would become Johannesburg. The years that followed brought several modest strikes, but the Witwatersrand Main Reef eluded searchers until 1886, when George Harrison, an Australian prospector, chanced upon an outcropping on a farm called Langlaagte. Ironically, Harrison failed to appreciate the significance of his find: he sold his claim for

£10 and embarked for the goldfields of the eastern Transvaal region.

Others were more farsighted. By mid-1886 an army of diggers had descended on the Witwatersrand, hacking away with picks and shovels along a line that soon stretched 40 miles west to east. In response to this influx, the government of the Transvaal, the small Boer republic under whose jurisdiction the Witwatersrand fell, dispatched two men, Vice President Christiaan Johannes Joubert and Deputy Surveyor-General Johann Rissik, to inspect the goldfields and identify a suitable city site. The new city was called Johannesburg, apparently in their honour.

As the scale of the gold deposits became apparent, Johannesburg became the 19th century's last great boomtown. Fortune hunters from as far afield as

Australia and California joined skilled Cornish and Welsh miners, who brought to South Africa a strong trade-union tradition. Destitute Afrikaners, driven from their rural homes by debt and drought, clustered in slums such as Brickfields and Vrededorp. Blacks from every corner of the southern African subcontinent migrated to the city, often in large ethnic cohorts, adding a dozen more voices to the cultural and linguistic babel. Most blacks worked on the mines, completing six- and nine-month contracts before returning to their rural homes. Others settled permanently in the swelling city, carving out niches as rickshaw drivers, domestic workers, and washermen. By 1896 Johannesburg had become a city of 100,000 people.

Conceived in avarice, the young city nurtured every species of vice. Banks and boardinghouses jostled for space with more than 500 saloons.

Criminal syndicates with roots in New York City and London found fertile soil in Johannesburg. The predominantly male population provided a robust market for prostitution. "Ancient Ninevah and Babylon have been revived," a visiting journalist wrote in 1913. "Johannesburg is their twentieth century prototype. It is a city of unbridled squalor and unfathomable squander."

Consolidation of the gold industry

The gold deposits of the Main Reef, for all their uncanny dependability, were also extremely low-grade. Tons of the pebbly conglomerate had to be mined, crushed, amalgamated with mercury (later cyanide), and retorted in order to produce even an ounce or two of gold. This fact, combined with gold's internationally fixed price, produced a perennial problem of profitability, which increased exponentially as the reef dipped away to the south to depths of hundreds, and ultimately thousands, of feet. (South African gold mines would eventually reach depths of over two miles, making them far and away the deepest mines in the world.)

All these factors promoted a rapid consolidation of the industry. By the mid-1890s control of the entire Witwatersrand gold industry rested in the hands of a half-dozen massive mining houses, each of which commanded thousands of workers and millions of dollars in capital, most of it raised from investors in Europe and the United States. Control of these companies lay with a small number of so-called "Randlords," men such as Alfred Beit, Barney Barnato, and J.B. Robinson, who had made their fortunes on the Kimberley diamond fields and well understood the exigencies of large-scale industrial mining. Working under the auspices of the newly formed Chamber of Mines, the Randlords strove to establish the profitability of their industry by rationalizing production and relentlessly squeezing down costs, especially the cost of labour.

The national and international context

As the Randlords' power waxed, so did their frustration with the Transvaal government, which they regarded as too corrupt and inefficient to meet the needs of a modern industrial economy. Boer officials extracted hefty bribes and handed out valuable concessions on supplies to political allies. Worse, the Transvaal government seemed unable to enact or enforce the kind of discriminatory taxes and rigorous master-servant laws that the Randlords regarded as essential to their campaign to reduce black labour costs. As one exasperated industry expert put it, Boers lacked the ability "to understand capitalism, industrialisation and progress."

Mineowners' frustrations were stoked by British officials, many of whom were eager to see the goldfields brought within the orbit of the British Empire. (In the political economyof the day, a nation's strength was a direct function of its hard currency reserves, and the reserves of the Bank of England had fallen to ominously low levels.) In 1895, British officials tacitly endorsed the Jameson Raid, a coup attempt against the Transvaal government conceived by the mining magnate Cecil John Rhodes. When that failed, they seized on the plight of the "uitlanders" the foreign, mostly British, miners in Johannesburg, who were denied the right to vote under Transvaal law. In September 1899 the British government delivered an ultimatum to the Boers demanding the immediate enfranchisement of all (white) uitlanders. In October 1899 the South African War (also known as the Boer War) began. When the fighting ceased two and a half years later, the Transvaal and its sister republic, the Orange Free State, were colonies of the British Empire.

British troops entered Johannesburg unopposed in June 1900. The mines, left undamaged by retreating Boers, were back in operation by the end of 1901. As mineowners had hoped, the Transvaal's new imperial overlords were sensitive to the industry's needs, rescinding Boer tariffs and concessions and enacting onerous new taxes and a pass law explicitly designed to force blacks to accept employment at whatever wages whites were willing to pay. When these devices failed to produce a sufficient pool of cheap labour, imperial officials cooperated with the Chamber of Mines in the temporary importation of more than 60,000 Chinese indentured labourers. By the inauguration of the Union of South Africa in 1910, the gold industry rested on a firm financial footing.

The local level

Racist enactments

The first decades of the 20th century were a time of extensive social engineering as municipal authorities, influenced by new currents in eugenics and city planning, attacked what they took to be the sources of urban disorder. In 1904, blacks living near the city centre were forcibly relocated to Klipspruit, 10 miles southwest of town. As had happened in earlier removals in Cape Town and Port Elizabeth, the move was preceded by a plague scare and accomplished in the name of "sanitation," though it is difficult to see how the interests of sanitation were served at Klipspruit, a municipal sewerage farm.

Similarly strained justifications were used in ensuing decades to relocate not only blacks but Indians, Coloureds, and even poor whites. The process was facilitated by the ideology of segregation, which emerged in the first quarter of the 20th century as a kind of panaceafor South Africa's "race problem." The 1923 Natives (Urban Areas) Act, for example, defined urban blacks as "temporary sojourners," welcome only insofar as they ministered "to the wants of the white population." While Johannesburg never availed itself of the full range of powers the law afforded, it took advantage of the act to relocate thousands of blacks from slums and backyards in the city to black townships such as Alexandra or Western Areas or to the new development at Orlando East, the first piece in the vast urban jigsaw that would become Soweto. Pass and liquor raids became regular features of township life, as police strove to root out those who were "idle," "disorderly," or simply superfluous to the white economy.

Black protests

Blacks did not simply accede to racist enactments. They organized innumerable petitions and deputations in the early years of the 20th century, protesting what they regarded as a betrayal of the British tradition of equality before the law. Protest exploded into outright resistance in the last years of World War I. Ground between low wages and murderous wartime inflation, African railway and municipal workers in Johannesburg staged bitter strikes. An emboldened Transvaal Native Congress, the local affiliate of the South African Native National Congress (renamed African National Congress [ANC] in 1923), launched a major antipass campaign, leading to several violent clashes with police. In 1920, 70,000 black mineworkers struck for better wages and working conditions. Eventually the army was called out to march the strikers underground at bayonet point.

Challenge by white workers

As significant as such resistance was, the chief challenge to South Africa's political order in the early decades of the 20th century came from Johannesburg's white workers. By custom, whites performed all skilled labour in the mines (a practice enshrined in the "job colour bar" provisions of the 1911 Mines and Works Act), commanding in return wages 5 to 10 times higher than those earned by blacks. Mineowners, ever on the lookout for ways to reduce costs, challenged white workers on three separate occasions in 1907, 1913, and 1922 encountering violent resistance each time. In the last case, a plan to reduce the proportion of whites in the mine labour force touched off a general strike, which quickly escalated into a full-scale armed insurrection. White workers, marching under banners that proclaimed "Workers of the World Fight and Unite for a White South Africa," seized control of the entire city, surrendering only after the arrival of 20,000 troops and a sustained air and artillery bombardment. More than 200 people died in the "Rand Revolt," including 30 blacks murdered by strikers.

The transformations of the 1930s and '40s

In the 1930s and '40s Johannesburg was transformed by a massive in-migration of blacks from the countryside. Primarily a consequence of deteriorating conditions in rural reserves, black urbanization also reflected the increasing availability of employment in the Witwatersrand's rapidly growing secondary industries. Born of the exigencies of war and sustained through the 1920s by government tariffs, South African manufacturing industry exploded in the 1930s, especially in the boom years that followed the country's departure from the gold standard in 1933. By the early 1940s manufacturing had outstripped both mining and agriculture in terms of its contribution to the gross national product. Most of this development was focused in Johannesburg and in old East Rand mining communities such as Benoni, Boksburg, and Germiston, where the number of blacks employed in secondary industry soon exceeded the number working in the mines. Ominously for segregationists, a growing percentage of these workers were not migrants but permanently urbanized proletarians, living with wives and children.

The conflict between the imperatives of segregation and industrialization came to a head during World War II. With white workers off to the front and booming factories desperate for labour, the government of Prime Minister Jan Smuts suspended the operation of influx control on the Witwatersrand, unleashing a cataract of urbanization. Johannesburg's black population virtually doubled, to more than 400,000. With housing construction at a standstill, new arrivals were crammed into already overcrowded townships or into informal squatter camps thrown up wherever there was open space. Squalid, overcrowded conditions bred disease and vice, but they also spawned new forms of political consciousness and action, evident in bus boycotts in Alexandra, defiant squatter movements, and the rise of the militant African National Congress Youth League. (Among the founders of the league was a young Johannesburg apprentice attorney named Nelson Mandela.) A new wave of trade unionism spread among workers, culminating in the 1946 black mineworkers' strike.

Johannesburg, South Africa

Apartheid

Enforcing the system

These transformations were not lost on white political leaders. On the contrary, the future of Johannesburg and other South African cities became the central issue in the 1948 national election. Jan Smuts' United Party, while defending its commitment to white supremacy, argued that complete segregation was chimerical and that some permanent black urbanization was an inevitable consequence of economic development. The National Party of Daniel F. Malan, in contrast, warned that whites were being "swamped" and called for a forceful restoration of the old order. Malan dubbed his policy "apartheid."

Buoyed by a massive turnout of Afrikaner voters, the Nationalists secured a parliamentary majority, which they retained for the next 46 years. In that time they enacted a panoply of laws that specified where one could live, work, or attend school, all on the basis of race. The squatter camps that had sprung up around Johannesburg in the mid-1940s were bulldozed, as were established settlements that fell within areas now designated as "White." Sophiatown, home to many of South Africa's most celebrated writers and musicians, was removed starting in 1955. In its place rose a new white working-class suburb, which authorities dubbed Triomf Afrikaans for "triumph."

The 1960s in Johannesburg were, depending on one's point of view, the best of times or the worst of times. With oppositional movements banned, the National Party had a free hand to elaborate its vision of "grand apartheid." Between 1960 and 1980 close to four million blacks were forcibly relocated, including several hundred thousand from Johannesburg, to remote, desiccated

Bantustans (ethnic "homelands"). While careful not to impede the flow of labour to industry, state officials enforced pass laws with unprecedented rigour: in the quarter-century preceding the final repeal of influx control in 1986 the state prosecuted nearly 10 million pass offenses, an average of more than 1,000 per day. For whites, on the other hand, these years brought unimagined prosperity. Over the course of the 1960s the South African economy grew nearly 6 percent per annum, a rate exceeded only by Japan. Needless to say, most of the benefits accrued to whites, who rewarded the National Party with ever greater parliamentary majorities.

Apartheid's demise

Beneath apartheid's placid surface, however, lay seething discontent discontent that exploded, inevitably, in Johannesburg. On June 16, 1976, South African police fired on a group of Soweto students who were marching in protest against state plans to impose Afrikaans as a medium of instruction in black schools. The shooting ignited a massive popular uprising that raged for months and eventually spread to more than 80 cities across South Africa. Townships around Johannesburg exploded again in 1984, in response to the National Party's introduction of a new constitution that conceded limited franchise rights to Indians and Coloureds while excluding the black majority. Unrest continued to rage throughout the 1980s, despite the declaration of a state of emergency and the deployment of units of the South African Defence Force. These years also witnessed the revival of black trade union activity, registered in a wave of strikes and stayaways that periodically brought the economy of the Witwatersrand to a halt. This growing militancy, coupled with tightening international economic sanctions, helped propel South Africa's white rulers to the negotiating table, paving the way for the country's first democratic elections in 1994, in which the ANC was victorious.

Under the new ANC government, the Municipal Structures Act was passed into law in 1998, further integrating and regulating local government in Johannesburg and throughout the country. Crime, chronically a problem in Johannesburg, became particularly acute in the 1990s and early 2000s, as violence drove businesses from the city centre into its safer suburbs.

Tourism

Johannesburg, fondly known as Jo'burg or Jozi, is a dichotomy of culture, like much of South Africa itself. Despite the gaps, it proves to have a richness in history and new modern districts full of things to do. As the host of the 2010 World Cup, many areas have been revamped into cool spaces with new purpose. The people are friendly and the recent improvements in transportation help Johannesburg travel be a great addition to a South Africa visit.

The area gained its wealth originally from gold and diamond mining. It has grown to be the third-largest city on the African continent, and the only one not near a major body of water. The country has eleven national languages, and the city mirrors that diversity to a T. Though English is the most common, Zulu, Afrikaans, and Xhosa are spoken along with others. Travel to Johannesburg offers new experiences for every kind of traveler.

Visitor should also be advised to take caution. Avoid walking around alone in parts of town at night, and ask locals for the safest places to withdraw money. Take care of your belongings, and keep a wary eye.

Guide to Johannesburg

Sightseeing in Johannesburg what to see. Complete travel guide

Up to 1886 Johannesburg was a small town without anything outstanding or popular. The destiny of this settlement was changed by the European named George Harrison who found a rich gold mine on the territory of the town.

Starting from that time Johannesburg began developing rapidly and just 10 years later already 50 thousand of Europeans lived there. Today this is the largest megalopolis on the territory of South Africa, a famous industrial center and a popular resort. Johannesburg is surrounded by several satellites with each of them having its sights and places of interest, but you should start your exploration of the city from its unique buildings and cultural centers.

Exhibitions to mines and old towns built during the times of Gold Rush still remain the most popular attraction among tourists. Loose pit refuse heaps and mines are turned into museums that feature collections of equipment, historical items and documents. Old towns make up a huge museum under the open sky, where you can see houses of miners. Gold Reef City is considered the most popular miner settlement.

We simply cannot fail to mention Sun City town that has been created by skillful architects and is located in the center of an ancient volcano. All tourists interested in active rest and night entertainments should definitely visit this place. You will not find so many aqua parks, entertainment centers and discos in any other city of Republic of South Africa. Near Sun City is located another attraction Pilanesberg National Park that is a home to over 6 thousands of wild animals including the representatives from the so called "big quintuple" leopards, rhinoceroses, buffalos, elephants and lions. One more unique nature sight is 40 meters deep Sterkfontein Caves.

The city has many interesting architectural monuments. Near the famous restaurant Blue Elephant is the Baan Chinpracha, built in the early 20th century. Beautiful European furniture and works of art, which were specially delivered from various European countries and China, were used for its decoration. Now the ancient mansion is accessible to tourists for visiting. They can admire the hidden collection of antiques within its walls.

In the vicinity of Johannesburg is the ethnic village of Lesedi. It will be a great place to explore the culture and traditions of the indigenous population. On the territory of this village are the dwellings of the five main tribes of South Africa. Travelers in this open-air museum will have a lot of entertainment. They will be able to try on the national costumes of the leaders, learn how to play amazing musical instruments and take part in incredibly interesting rituals. Every day, there are interesting shows with music and dances for visitors of the village. Here you can also buy many interesting souvenirs.

Johannesburg, South Africa

Fans of theatrical art in Johannesburg should definitely visit the theater with the unusual name Market. It was built on a square where a large Indian market had previously been located. The opening of the theater took place at the end of the 20th century. In 1974 local theaters started raising funds for its construction. Now the original theater is the owner of a number of prestigious awards. It regularly hosts interesting productions, music concerts and other cultural events.

The perfect place for a family excursion will be the Observatory Ridge. It is located in the highest point of the city, on the top of the mountain range. The opening of this observatory took place back in 1903. Near the observatory is equipped with several wonderful observation platforms. So, after a cognitive excursion you can admire the panorama of the city.

An attraction known only to tourist units is the University of Witwatersrand. Its opening took place in 1896 and is one of the most majestic architectural monuments in the city. The building of the university is surrounded by a picturesque garden. Everyone can walk along it, and in the courtyard, admire the original landscape decorations.

Family trip with kids

Family trip to Johannesburg with children. Ideas on where to go with your child
In Johannesburg, there are many nature reserves, entertainment centers and attractions that children will surely like. One of the most interesting and visited is the Monte casino bird park. The main inhabitants of this park are exotic birds, among which there are dozens of species of parrots. Lovely monkeys and lemurs live in the

park. The park is very beautiful and interestingly decorated. There are artificial ponds on its territory, near to which peacocks are walking freely, and many equipped recreational areas with benches and tables.

For those who want to immerse themselves in a real world of wildlife, it is worth making a safari in the Lion and Rhino Nature Reserve. Lions and rhinoceroses live in this park. On its territory, interesting jeep safaris are conducted, and also visitors are offered a walk in the safest places and the opportunity to play with young lions. This is one of the few reserves in Africa where animals can be observed from as close as possible.

There is also a classic zoo in Johannesburg called Johannesburg. It is perfect for those who do not want to go far away from the city and expect to devote a few hours to excursion. In this zoo, one can see all the main representatives of the African fauna: elephants, rhinoceroses, zebras, cheetahs and lions. Quite exotic animals for Africa live in the zoo, including polar bears. Also in the zoo, there is a big and very interesting terrarium.

A wide selection of entertainment and sports centers is available for holidaymakers, among which there is a suitable one for the youngest travelers and even for adolescents. Everyone, including travelers with children will like the entertainment center Bounce Inc. It is an indoor center and it offers its visitors a world-wide catching entertainment - trampolines. Here one can just jump and sharpen his acrobatic skill, or play various sports games on the trampolines. This entertainment center is equally popular among both children and adults.

With older children, one can visit the Tree Top Adventures. It was opened in a picturesque park area and offers guests very unusual entertainment and attractions. Here one can ride a bungee, walk along rope bridges among tree, go through various obstacle courses and labyrinths. In the park, suitable attractions will be found for both young children and adults. It will be an ideal place for a family holiday.

There are excellent museums in Johannesburg, which are also worth visiting with children. One of the most original is the Sci-Bono Discovery Center. In this museum, there are no boring halls with showcases of exhibits that cannot be touched, all expositions are interactive. During the excursion, children will be able to learn how electricity is produced, how the basic laws of physics manifest themselves in nature and how a unique human organism is arranged. The museum will also be interesting for adults, because they will be able to learn about the latest achievements of science.

Johannesburg is full of entertainments fans of outdoor activities. In addition to traditional cycling and horseback riding there are also some very original ways to spend leisure time. Balloon tours are very popular among travelers with children. They are organized by many tourist centers. Ballooning is one of the best ways to appreciate the unique beauty of African nature.

Cuisine & restaurants

Cuisine of Johannesburg for gourmets. Places for dinner best restaurants
Every restaurant in Johannesburg is able to surprise visitors by plenty of signature treats. Meat and game prepared according to national recipes are especially popular with holidaymakers. Another distinctive feature of the local cuisine is a

rich selection of wines that will be the best complement to your favorite dishes. The Butcher Shop & Gril restaurant offers its visitors a great choice of dishes cooked on a grill. Steak in considered the signature dish of this dining facility. In addition to it visitors should definitely choose one of original vegetable garnishes.

Ciao Baby Succina restaurant is a very attractive place that is famous not only because of a rich choice of various dishes, but also because of very reasonable prices. Fans of seafood should not forget to order soup with mussels. Do not forget to try the local pizza it is definitely worth your attention. Continue tasting delicious seafood dishes in Ocean Basket restaurant. Fish and shellfish are cooked in accordance with special recipes that include interesting and unusual spices. Therefore, the food offered here is simply delicious.

People who cannot imagine a meal without meat will be glad to visit Smith & Wollensky restaurant. Rich choice of venison, steaks and traditional food cooked on an open fire simply every visitor will easily find here dishes to fit one's taste. Fratelli Pizzeria restaurant specializes in cooking dishes from Italian cuisine. Every day this cozy restaurant attracts numerous fans of pizza. It is also very popular among vegetarians.

McGinty's pub is one of the most unique institutions of the city. It's simply impossible to distinguish it from institutions that can be found in Ireland. Wide choice of different sorts of beer, salads and light snacks attract numerous locals and visitors to this cozy and warm pub. On weekends McGinty's always organizes interesting musical performances. Fans of Japanese cuisine should not forget to visit Go Sushi restaurant. During the daytime visitors are welcome to order a business lunch at most attractive price.

Montego Bay restaurant should be definitely mentioned when it comes to describing prestigious dining facilities of the city. The basis of its menu is represented by rare and unique signature seafood dishes. The hall of the restaurant is distinguished by pleasant festive atmosphere. The restaurant will be a perfect choice for various parties and banquets. Sweet tooth tourists will find all they need and more in La Mill cafe. Every day the café's bakers delight visitors with new cakes and pastries. Guests will be pleasantly surprised at not only a great selection of sweets, but also reasonable prices.

Tashas, between cafe and fine dining
With a hybrid concept in Johannesburg, Thashas is a modern and laid back cafe that offers fresh and

innovative recipes for breakfast, lunch, or just a gourmet break.

From the moment you step in, the rows of pastries exposed under the glass windows really catch the eye. Above your head, old books have been customised and turned into chandeliers. In the Rosebank neighbourhood of Johannesburg, Tashas is always packed, just like the 9 other restaurants of the franchise in town. They are all themed and, here, influences hark back to Manhattan's trendy cafes. From the stylish decoration, stripped-down and bright, to the huge black counter, everything screams New York. Food lovers come any time of the day for brunch, lunch or just a snack. The very varied menu takes on the healthy-eating trend, with high-protein smoothies and *steel-cut oats*(with yogurt, maple syrup, caramelised bananas, almonds, coconut and cinnamon) perfect for tea time. The most ravenous ones will gladly indulge in the *Tashas hotchoc*, chocolate-based hot drink served with marshmallows. The perfect snack.

Tashas
Shop No. G28, The Zone, Oxford Rd
Rosebank
Johannesburg 2196
+27 (0)11 447 7972

Perron, Johannesburg's Mexican touch

When Mexico and South Africa meet, the result is Perron Melville.

The owners brought Mexico back to Johannesburg and endeavour with great enthusiasm to make it known on a daily basis through their typical yet original cuisine. No *fajitas* here, for instance. In this third Perron restaurant of the South African metropolis, located in the trendy Melville neighbourhood, turquoise and fuchsia tones are to be found everywhere, as they give the place its laid back feel. The impression of entering an Aztec territory is incredible, as it remains 14,000 kilometres away. Walls and accessories are as colourful as the menu itself, mainly offering tapas to share, original *tacos*, *ceviche*, *nacho* platters and *quesadillas*. During the summer, enjoy the outdoor terrace and sip on a cocktail, like a coriander and jalapeño margarita. Then sit up to indulge in a few *Los Mas Pequenos*, a platter of shareable dishes, perfect with family or friends. For a few minutes, let your mind wander over the Atlantic Ocean all the way to Mexico and explore its flavours.

Perron Melville
65 4th Avenue
Melville, Gauteng
Johannesburg 2109
+27 (0)11 482 1215

A truly unique brunch at Salvation Café

Johannesburg, South Africa

In a warm and relaxing setting, Salvation Café presents a very original menu for breakfast, entirely homemade.

Written in chalk on a black board, you will discover Salvation Café's slogan: "Non-pretentious food, prepared with love". In the heart of the trendy Milpark neighbourhood in Johannesburg, this coffee shop is packed at brunch time, most patrons making the trip to enjoy the house speciality: eggs. Benedict with or without smoked salmon and avocado, Florentine with or without spinach... there is something for everyone.

Take a seat on the terrace, genuine haven of rest, with iron-wrought chairs displayed around the fountain and bench seats covered with large blue pillows. The perfect setting to enjoy a homemade ice tea (pineapple, ginger or lemon). In addition to the eggs, the menu offers a large selection of dishes to please the palate. Choose the French toast in savoury form with halloumi typically Cypriot cheese pesto and cherry tomatoes, or the brunch burrito with eggs, guacamole, tomato sauce and beef sausage or halloumi depending on your taste. The best way to start off the day with a hearty breakfast!

Salvation Café
44 Stanley Avenue
Milpark
Johannesburg 2092
+27 (0)11 482 7795

Turn 'n Tender: real meat from a real family

Make the most of delicious steaks in a friendly atmosphere.

Founded by four brothers in 1977, this family institution now has eight establishments, including those in Parktown North, Bassonia, Illovo, and Bryanston.

Johannesburg, South Africa

They are known to offer the best choice of prime meats in Johannesburg. The house specialty remains the steak and you can try one of the four special variations created by the four brothers. You can also opt for any of a variety of cuts and specialty toppings, ranging from chimichurri, an Argentine marinade, to bordelaise or mushrooms and feta. You can also decide on pure beef burgers, ribs, lamb, game, or seafood. Don't miss the biltong, the South African dried and cured meat specialty. A rich wine list will highlight the flavours of your chosen meal.

The team is always ready to offer advice, with passion and professionalism, to the delight of numerous regulars. If you like meat, you are in the right place.

Turn'n Tender
Parktown Quarter

22 3rd Avenue
Johannesburg 2193
+27 (0)11 788 7933

The Butcher Shop and Grill

For meat lovers, this is a South African institution.

If you like very tender and delicious steak, a stop here is a must. Installed on Nelson Mandela Square in Sandton, you won't be alone in a restaurant that seats 600, but an army of waiters will take good care of you. The setting is classic, with an emerald green ceiling, wooden chairs, and crisp, white tablecloths.

The owner, who comes from a family of butchers, knows what he sells. The perfectly selected cuts are cooked to taste and accompanied by a multitude of sauces and original side dishes. They highly recommend not overcooking your chosen steak, as South African meats are much lower in fat than meats in Europe and the US. Twenty tonnes of steak are served every month here. The menu also offers lamb, pork, and seafood, but takes little account of vegetarians.

An excellent choice of wines is on hand to accompany the great dishes. With panoramic views of the square, you'll feel like Johannesburg is right on your plate. Here the food is authentic and you can tell.

The Butcher Shop and Grill
Shop 30, Nelson Mandela Square
Sandton 2196
+27 (0)11 784 8676

Sakhumzi

The best address for a delicious, hearty lunch in Soweto.

Sakhumzi awaits you on the famous Vilakazi Street, the heart of the historical and cultural centre of

Soweto and the only street in the world where two Nobel Peace Prize winners used to live: Desmond Tutu and Nelson Mandela. A former shebeen, an illegal bar during apartheid, it is now a traditional restaurant that is very appreciated by the population of the district.

On the menu, some Zulu or Xhosa dishes such as mielie pap (mashed maize), xushu (beans and maize kernels) served with a mutton stew, morogo (wild spinach), dombolo (a steam-baked bread), and umngqusho (maize served with beans), one of Nelson Mandela's favourite dishes. You can also opt for a stew, a curry, grilled meats, snacks, or salads. Lunch at the picnic tables on a shaded terrace outside, and take in the ambience of this famous district.

Sakhumzi
6980 Vilakazi Street
Soweto 1804

Johannesburg, South Africa

+27 (0)11 536 1379

Moyo: the place for hip gourmets

The Melrose Arch neighbourhood is the place for the famous Moyo restaurant, known for its funky concerts and electric ambiance.

With its terrace and its five levels, this immense and fashionable spot gives you an idea of the ambiance of the chic areas of Johannesburg. Found in other big South African cities as well, this inescapable chain restaurant has several establishments that are archetypes of the new 'rainbow' generation in South Africa.

Traditional fine cuisine that is revisited with a twist, a solid wine list, and an artsy setting with original contemporary design are on offer. Curry tagines from Mozambique sidle up to South African seafood the whole continent is on stage and brought to your table for you to taste. You can also head out to the terrace and its stylized wrought iron chairs, a cocktail in hand, to watch the crowd on big nights out. The place is also famous for its music, which mixes jazz and itinerant mbira (thumb piano) players from Zimbabwe.

The property revels in beautifully lit interiors, cosy alcoves, and earth tones throughout. The ensemble gives it an irresistible African urban style that has merited it the appreciation of many customers. A reference and a gourmet stop not to be missed.

Moyo
5, The High Street
Melrose Arch
Johannesburg 2076
+27 (0)11 684 1477

Kitchener's Carvery Bar

Johannesburg, South Africa

The perfect place for a glass in an authentic setting with a cool ambiance.

After a long day, here at Kitchener's you can enjoy homemade cocktails with music piped in the background. This bar has been open on the first floor of a two-story Dutch house for slightly more than a century.

With period decor, the place is where the trendy youth of Johannesburg meet up and a must if you're looking for a quirky bar open until all hours of the night. Located in the Milner Hotel in the heart of downtown Johannesburg, Kitchener's has cotton tapestries, embossed tin ceilings, and mosaic floors that make the bar feel like a time capsule. Known for its refreshing eclecticism, it enjoys a musical reputation that lives up to its impressive history. You can enjoy cocktails in the bar or dance to live tunes many nights.

If you're lucky, you may get to see an improvised session by a well-known artist come to 'slum it up', away from prying eyes.

Kitchener's Carvery Bar
71 Juta Street
Johannesburg 2000
+27 (0)11 403 0166

44 Stanley

Abandoned industrial buildings from the 1930s have been transformed into design studios, galleries, and restaurants.

Along Empire Road, a virtual border between the rich districts of the north and the poor neighbourhoods of the south, awaits a new type of mall, with a very New York feel.

Brian Green bought this large complex of abandoned and dilapidated 1930s warehouses in 2003. The former film director rehabilitated them into a mini-village with a huge courtyard where trendy restaurants coexist with vanguard shops and street art. At 44 Stanley, you will only see local designers, shops, and restaurants, in contrast to many shopping centres dedicated to mass consumption. There are some lovely terraces here too.

A young clientele and families wander about the stalls or share a meal on a central square that brings Provence to mind. Make sure you see Jonathan Robinson: he roasts fair trade coffee on location that has been imported from several African countries, such as Ethiopia, Kenya, and Rwanda, among others.

44 Stanley
44 Stanley Avenue
Johannesburg 2092
+27 (0)11 482 4444

Traditions & lifestyle

Colors of Johannesburg traditions, festivals, mentality and lifestyle

Johannesburg is one of the most populous cities in the country. The city has become home to representatives of different nationalities. Foreign tourists will be particularly interested in culture and lifestyle of the ethnic tribes. However, when dealing with the indigenous people, tourists should take into account a lot of important points. The locals have rather different approach to Europeans. Many of the natives simply prefer to avoid them and show their feelings quite openly. Others, however, can express increased interest and attention to foreigners.

When communicating with the local residents tourists should not be aggressive. They need to be friendly and quite restrained. It also is not recommended to photograph the local people without their permission, as well as to try to enter someone's home without invitation. If the local people do not feel any threat or aggression from the side of foreigners, they will behave in a very friendly and open manner.

When it comes to clothes, there are no strict rules here. Classic and casual styles of clothes are very appropriate, but tourists shouldn't wear khaki colored clothes. Wearing accessories, clothes and shoes in military style is simply not accepted here. Even children are not allowed to wear such outfits. Residents of the city usually prefer European style of clothes, but people in small tribal villages located in the outskirts of the city can wear national costumes and very specific headgear.

In no case should travellers express their surprise and discuss national costumes in public. This can become the reason for offence. The locals are quite sociable and are always happy to share the latest news with visitors and tell them about the art of local crafts. However, when dealing with the indigenous people travellers should certain avoid some "taboos".

Do not criticize their way of life and customs and never show your dissatisfaction with the local regulations. Political situation in the country is also not the best topic for a conversation, as well as relationship between the local people and migrants from European countries. By following several simple rules tourists can easily protect themselves from numerous adverse situations and make their rest very comfortable. During excursions and sightseeing programs tourists need to listen to guides carefully, as they will surely tell visitors about the rules of behavior and cultural characteristics of Johannesburg.

Culture: sights to visit

Culture of Johannesburg. Places to visit - old town, temples, theaters, museums and palaces

A beautiful modern city with rich historical heritage, every year Johannesburg attracts numerous travelers from around the world. The center of the city is the most attractive area for walking. This is also the location of a significant part of excursion sites. Johannesburg is often called "the city of gold" because it was founded around a famous mine, in which gold mining was carried out during several decades.

Today the gold mine has been converted into an open air museum. This historical part of the city is called Gold Reef City. During an excursion here guests will be offered to go down into a deep pit and watch the how gold is mined and processed. There is an interesting shop in the territory of the museum. Here anyone can buy ancient and modern gold coins.

The city is home to a huge number of various museums and theaters. For example, Market Theatre Cultural Center is known far beyond the borders of the country. Here are located three theaters, art galleries, as well as several restaurants, nightclubs and bars. This is a unique entertainment complex that is perfect for relaxing and having fun every day.

Guests of the city should definitely not forget to visit Museum of Africa, which will help visitors to get acquainted with history and culture of the local people. The museum often hosts interesting workshops and lectures. In addition to the permanent exhibition of historical artifacts, visitors of the museum are welcome to see the works of contemporary artists. Art Gallery is a truly outstanding cultural institution. Here visitors can see a rich collection of paintings by African and European artists. Many works of art were created more than one hundred years ago. In the gallery you will find famous works by Pablo Picasso, Claude Monet, Edgar Degas, and other legendary artists.

There is also Sculpture Park not far away from the gallery. This place is also worth visiting as it features a unique collection of works of art. Any holiday program should include a visit to National Museum of Military History. The biggest part of its exposition is dedicated to military equipment, which was seized by the South Africans during the war in Angola. During your walk through the central area of the city you can see a lot of beautiful historic buildings that border with modern skyscrapers and elegant business centers.

This contrast makes Johannesburg even more charming and attractive to foreign tourists

Attractions & nightlife

City break in Johannesburg. Active leisure ideas for Johannesburg - attractions, recreation and nightlife

Johannesburg attracts fans of ecotourism as various safaris and walks in the local nature reserves remain the most popular form of entertainment. Sterkfontein Caves are one of the most important natural attractions of the region. The system of caves includes six deep caverns, the minimum depth of which is 40 meters. There is a beautiful lake in one cavern, and another one has become a real boon for archaeologists. During an excursion to the caves visitors will hear about all their secrets. Guided tours to Sterkfontein are offered every day.

Johannesburg, South Africa

Tourists who want to learn the culture and customs of the local people will be interested in visiting the village of Lesedi. Participants in this excursion will be able to see real African homes and watch fascinating rituals and beautiful dance performances. The most famous natural reserve of Johannesburg, Lions Garden, is a great place to make a memorable and interesting walk.

The reserve has got its name not by an accident - its territory is inhabited by several families of lions. There are also more than 20 other species of the local fauna in the reserve. This place is also the location of a beautiful grotto Miracle Cave. The age of the grotto is more than two million years. An excursion to the reserve lasts more than four hours and includes visits to all the most important natural attractions.

Besides famous gold mines there is a large diamond mine called Premier in the city. This is the place where the world's largest diamond has been found. Nowadays the mine is free for public visits. The main inhabitants of Magaliesberg Nature Reserve are elephants. Vacationers will be surely delighted with a unique opportunity to take photos with young elephants, watch interesting performances even ride an elephant through the picturesque countryside.

Tourists should definitely not forget to visit the local zoo that is known as one of the most famous zoos in the world. The area of the zoo is approximately 600 acres, and its territory is home to approximately 3.5 thousand of exotic animals and birds. There is a funicular road above the zoological park. Enjoying the beauty of this place from the bird's eye has become a popular pastime among tourists. A significant part of large shopping centers, night clubs and restaurants is located in the central area of the city. Market Theatre is an original entertainment center, where interesting theater performances, music concerts and other events take place literary every day

Art Cultural sights

Afrikaner heritage and a newly named urban area

The former fiefdom of white domination has been renamed Tshwane, though the administrative area retains the name Pretoria. An indispensable stop on the quest to understanding the country's history.

With its avenues lined with thousands of jacaranda trees and its imposing architecture, Pretoria remains a crucial place for understanding the political history of South Africa.

The administrative capital of the country includes important historical monuments such as the Union Building, the seat of government where Nelson Mandela gave his inaugural address in 1994, and the Voortrekker Monument, a tribute to Afrikaner history. Elsewhere, there is the courthouse, with its beautiful facade adorned with balconies, the location of Mandela's 1963 treason trial that ended with his life sentence. There is also the home of the iconic Paul Kruger, a former president of the Transvaal.

Among other things, Pretoria hosts the largest university in the country, the Pretoria Art Museum and its fine collection of traditional and contemporary art, and the National Zoological Gardens. This 80-hectare space is home to vast enclosures of more than 2,500 representatives of the local fauna, an aquarium, a vivarium, and a splendid collection of exotic trees.

Zulu art

A passionate artist dedicated to preserving the wealth of a civilisation that is disappearing.

Founded by artist Kim Sacks, an accomplished ceramist who has travelled the world to study the craft, this amazing gallery showcases the work of local and international artists from all over Africa.

Here you will see a collection of ceramics and quality South African objects devoutly gathered by Sacks, who fights tirelessly for a civilization in great danger of dying. A woman with white skin but the heart of Zulu, steeped in passion and tenderness, Kim loves the creative genius of humanity.

Stop for a moment or for a few hours, and browse the extensive collection. Why not buy a unique piece of art? There are wooden carvings from the Congo, Zulu pottery, Mauritanian furniture, the threads and beads of South Africa, plus the textiles and ceramics of many artists on display here. A bright, peaceful, and harmonious space, it offers rare and unusual objects of great beauty.

Kim Sacks Gallery

153 Jan Smuts Avenue

Parkwood

Johannesburg 2193

+27 (0)11 447 5804

Cradle of Humankind: a remarkable paleontological site

An immense 50,000-hectare area, declared a UNESCO World Heritage Site in 1999, this is one of the most important palaeontological sites in the world.

Excavated since the 1930s, this site has already delivered precious treasures from the dawn of humanity, including remarkably preserved

Australopithecus skeletons, the oldest dating from about 3.5 million years ago, making it among the oldest humanoid remains ever uncovered.

Excavations continue and discoveries are made almost daily here in the Sterkfontein Valley, about a half-hour drive from Johannesburg. A prehistoric site of major importance in the world, it is composed of some forty limestone caves, including the Sterkfontein, one of only two that you can visit, where nearly a third of the hominid fossils in the world have been discovered.

Declared a World Heritage Site by UNESCO, the Cradle has a recently refurbished visitors centre and now offers you an educational centre, as well. Take a stroll and visit the galleries and underground streams. Academic experts will show you current dig sites via guided tours, letting you peek inside and examine the rocky walls.

Caleb Gray

Cradle of Humankind
Gauteng
+27 (0)11 085 2500

Soweto: victory against apartheid

The township that is a historical symbol of the fall of apartheid has now become a truly modern city with trendy restaurants and a huge shopping centre.

Designated by its geographical position in the south-west of the city, South West Township (So-we-to) remains the historic district that saw the rise of the ANC, Mandela, and Desmond Tutu, and the fall of apartheid. This renowned township is a place of memory today and you can visit with different tour operators who will show you the sites on a bicycle or in a bus. The house where Nelson Mandela lived in 1962, before his decades-long imprisonment, has now become a museum.

Johannesburg, South Africa

Strolling before the pictures, and among the Spartan furniture and everyday objects, you take in the fragments of a poignant saga and can perhaps imagine the family taking refuge under a table while police launch tear gas outside. Just a few metres away, the villa of Desmond Tutu neighbours that of Winnie Mandela.

To add to this concentration of history, visit the Hector Pieterson Memorial and Museum, named after the 12-year-old schoolboy who was shot in the back during the events of 1976 known as the 'Soweto Uprising' or '16 June'. That day, the police fired on the crowd, killing 23 people. This tragedy marked the beginning of the end of apartheid.

Mandela House
8115 Vilakazi Street & Ngakane Street
Johannesburg 1804
+27 (0)11 936 7754

Museum Africa: national history on display

A museum that treats the history and culture of the country with panache.

Located in the halls of a former fruit and vegetable market in the Newlands, Museum Africa, dedicated to the social and cultural history of South Africa, features vaulted exhibition spaces that occupy an entire block. Through its paintings, photographs, and wonderful exhibits, take a journey that fascinates both children and adults curious to learn more about the industrial heritage, culture, and history of the country. Want a preview of what you find here?

The history of Gauteng and Johannesburg, the first sites in the discovery of gold, plus reconstructions of townships and the interiors of residences. There are also presentations of South African music, with its most representative instruments, photography and cinema, and cave art in a reconstructed cavern. Another area is dedicated to Gandhi's life in Johannesburg and yet another on the historic 1956 trial of anti-apartheid militants.

Museum Africa
Lilian Ngoyi Street
Johannesburg 2000
+27 (0)11 833 5624

Goodman Gallery

For several decades, this gallery has been the place to see both new and acclaimed artists.

At the forefront of contemporary art in South Africa, the Goodman Gallery showcases South African artists, while including others from across the continent. Founded in 1966, at the time of apartheid, in the Parkwood neighbourhood by Linda Goodman, the gallery played a considerable role in the emergence of young black artists who were then denied access to galleries and museums.

Photography from the apartheid era was synonymous with political struggle. The artists of the country were engaged in a radical fight against segregationist policies, using art as their weapon. Through their testimonies and art works, they tried to counter the inequality. The top South African photographer, David Goldblatt, represented by the Goodman Gallery, has put his country on film, especially the city of Johannesburg.

Do not hesitate to discover the Goodman; the contemporary South African photography scene is now one of the most dynamic in the world, and its representatives have gained international recognition. Rightly so.

Goodman Gallery

163 Jan Smuts Avenue

Johannesburg 2193

From Constitution Hill to Carlton Centre

Visit the vestiges of colonial South Africa on Constitution Hill before heading up to the top floor of the city's tallest building for a breath-taking 360º view of Johannesburg.

In the area of Johannesburg called Braamfontein, Constitution Hill contains a collection of modern and historical buildings. The Old Fort Prison is a former military fort that had become a prison, primarily for white prisoners; it is now a museum. The 'Number Four' section contained more than 2,200 prisoners in a space constructed for 979 including famous 'guests' like Nelson and Winnie Mandela, and Gandhi. Also to be found are the

Constitutional Hall, a courthouse with contemporary public art and the Constitutional Court, the highest court of law in the country.

A 15-minute drive away on Commissioner Street, the Carlton Centre, with its 50 floors, can be spotted from a distance. It houses a mall and a panoramic bar, called Top of Africa, and a rooftop terrace, overlooking the city lights, that can accommodate up to 450 guests for an elegant dinner, concert, or fashion show. Be aware that visits on foot are best for the daytime as the streets empty very quickly on Constitution Hill in the late afternoon and evening.

Constitution Hill
11 Kotze Street
Braamfontein
Johannesburg 2107
+27 (0)11 381 3100

David Krut Projects: front-row culture

Johannesburg, South Africa

Bookstore, exhibition space, print workshop, and more, the alternative arts institution David Krut Projects works with contemporary South African art and artists in myriad ways.

Renowned for its temporary exhibitions and its many art publications available in limited editions, the David Krut Projects arts initiative, which now has a New York branch, allows you to take the pulse of the arts scene while deepening your African cultural knowledge.

The organization has an experimental workshop, the David Krut Print Workshop, in which artists can create freely: Among those who have worked here are Godfried Donkor, Senzo Shabangu, Maja Maljevic, Mary Wafer, William Kentridge, Jürgen Partenheimer, Cannonball Press, Robyn Penn, Chris Cozier, Stephen Hobbs, Nathaniel Sheppard, and Chad Cordeiro.

Interest in South African art is growing, thanks to the work of the Museum of Contemporary Art Africa, which focuses on contemporary artists and supports collections, which was far from the case in the past. The relaxed atmosphere of this elegant place of creation is particularly popular with the trendy minds of Johannesburg.

David Krut Projects
151 Jan Smuts Avenue
Johannesburg 2193
+27 (0)11 880 5646

Tips for tourists

Preparing your trip to Johannesburg: advices & hints - things to do and to obey

1. Tourists are recommended to use only bottled water for drinking. You can find it in all grocery stores and supermarkets. Tap water is not harmful to health, but the use of it can exacerbate the process of acclimatization.

2. Tourists should make excursions around the city only when accompanied with a guide or in a group. Soweto, Alexandra, Hillbrow and Kettlhong are considered the most unsafe areas for walking and sightseeing.

3. Tourists, who plan to travel around the city by car, in no case should stop in solitary places and leave their car unattended. If during your journey you see the «DO NOT STOP!» sign, this means that drivers are allowed not to stop even if there's a red stoplight.

4. All valuable items should be stored in your guestroom's safe. When going out, it is recommended not to wear jewelry and watches. Cellphones are advised to wear inside a bag and not in your hand. Any valuable item can attract thieves.

5. Holiday-makers are not recommended to use public transport. There are many special tour buses that ply around the city every day. Travellers can also get a taxi or rent a car with ease.

6. Smoking and consuming alcohol is prohibited in public areas. Violators of this rule will be charged heavy fines. Appearance on the streets of the city in a drunken state may also be the reason for a monetary penalty.

7. Travelers, who expect to dedicate much time to shopping, are recommended to pay in cash. When using a credit card, tourists are likely to become victims of fraud. It is also better to ask money in small denominations in banks and exchange offices. This way there will be no need to exchange large bills in shops and markets when you make purchases.

8. Tips are not officially accepted in restaurants and bars of the city, but any monetary reward will be appropriate. As a rule, a tip of 10% of the total order is enough.

9. The periods from the beginning of December to the end of January and from July to September are considered the high season. At that time, prices in hotels, restaurants and shops are always increased substantially.

10. items made of precious and semi-precious stones and jewelry remain one of the most popular souvenirs with tourists. The best way to purchase jewelry is to visit specialty stores. Tourists are not recommended to buy expensive items from individuals and sellers at market

Shopping in Johannesburg

Shopping in Johannesburg - authentic goods, best outlets, malls and boutiques

The most interesting place for shopping in Johannesburg is Neighbourgoods Market. This market is located in a cozy alley and is not easy to be found. They sell great products, inexpensive clothes and beautiful handmade souvenirs around here. Many tourists come to this market especially to enjoy refreshing drinks and try out street food. You can always enjoy its lively atmosphere, the sounds of music and the noisy speech of locals are heard everywhere.

In search of memorable gifts, you can go to African Craft Market of Rosebank, which houses numerous artisan workshops. If you're not lucky to find appropriate souvenirs, local masters will fulfill your individual order right there. Their prices are the most attractive in the city.

Johannesburg, South Africa

Budget tourists should definitely come by Pick n'Pay grocery store. It will be interesting to gourmets and can become an excellent alternative to local restaurants. In this store, the most popular products are sold. A one-liter juice box costs only 7 - 8 rand. They always have a large choice of cheese, sausages, and fresh bread. You can purchase popular dishes to take away, as well.

Ladies will like Ryash Fashion women's clothing store. It is one of the most expensive and prestigious in the city. There are very few visitors in the store. Its main customers are wealthy tourists. Here, you can choose clothes of different styles, including very beautiful dresses, at a cost about 700 rands. They have also beautiful business clothes. 400 - 500 rands is a price to be paid for excellent jackets. All the goods are of the highest quality.

If there's a Spar store on your way around the city, make sure to visit it. This is a large and popular supermarket, which is distinguished by a huge assortment of goods and affordable prices. Visitors can always choose fresh bread, ready-made salads, sweets and other popular dishes to take away. It has a large non-food department, as well.

Among the shopping centers of Johannesburg, Sandton City is worth noting. It is nice for a family visit. The center has a lot of clothing stores for every taste, restaurants, and cafes. Various attractions are equipped there for children. The center includes jewelry salons, giftware, and even stores that sell winter clothes. Some pavilions offer fabulous souvenirs in African style.

Eastgate shopping center will pleasantly surprise with a variety of stores, as well. Not only clothes can be chosen here. This complex will appeal to active tourists and sports fans. It presents first-class sports shops. Ladies can attend cosmetics and perfumery stores, and shops that offer household goods. There are also several grocery stores and a café with affordable prices.

On the territory of the picturesque park is a very beautiful and unusual Fourways Farmers Market. They sell not only products. Upscale cooks, who create masterpieces using simple and affordable products, work here. There are tables and chairs everywhere on the market, so you can enjoy wonderful national food all day long. Children and grown-ups will be delighted by a huge number of sandwiches, meat deep-fried, seafood, fruit cocktails and salads.

The Mall of Rosebank is a perfect gastronomic destination. It presents dozens of kinds of sweet treats, salads, potato chips and other delicacies.

The Mall includes many excellent clothing stores and souvenir pavilions, as well

Why Johannesburg Is Becoming Africa's Hippest City

Within a converted warehouse in what used to be one of the most dangerous parts of Johannesburg, you can eat gelato made by an Italian who had the machines shipped over from his family's store in Rome. You can taste golden fish from Mozambique cooked in the Congolese style, with rice and plantains, sample corn cakes with four kinds of sauce made by a Zulu bohemian who describes his style of dress as "funky Amish," or try ginger roti made by Rastafarians who, when you ask where they hail from, will tell you they are citizens of the "celestial paradise of the fifth dimension."

Nearby, on a rooftop, you can dance to salsa music. On the street below, you can watch a drunken Frenchman wave his hands like a rhythmically challenged conductor while musicians play marimbas made from wooden pallets. Around the block, as techno from Zimbabwe rattles the speakers of a car parked nearby, you can meet a jeweler from one of the townships who used to get the brass for his rings by melting down discarded kerosene stoves, but now makes pieces out of silver and gold for the affluent shoppers who roam the neighborhood.

That's how it always is on Sundays at Market on Main, in Maboneng, a neighborhood I'm pretty sure is unlike any other in Africa or the world. Some people may tell you it's like New York City's Williamsburg or Los Feliz in L.A., but in comparison with Maboneng, the forces of change in those places move at the pace of continental plates. Ten years ago, Maboneng didn't exist. I don't mean it wasn't yet trendy. I mean the name hadn't been invented. If you had walked through the area then and you would not have walked through the area then you likely would have seen abandoned warehouses that had been "hijacked" by criminals who extorted punishing rents from people living without running water or electricity, five to a room. Almost everyone with money lived and worked out in the suburbs, behind steel barricades and electric fences.

Most tourists to Johannesburg would stay in the suburbs, too. They rarely saw much of the city, except what they happened to glimpse through the windows of the car taking them between their hotel and the airport, which connects the wonders of southern Africa to the rest of the world. Until recently, people didn't come to Johannesburg to visit Johannesburg. They came on their way to the dunes of the Namib, or Botswana's Okavango Delta, or the wine country outside Cape Town. The

Johannesburg, South Africa

goal was to get in and out of the city as fast as possible.

Today, skipping the city would be a mistake. Johannesburg is as dynamic and exciting as any place I've been. Apartheid scarred South Africa and cut it off from most of the rest of the world, and corruption and crime do still plague the country. But although South Africa faces serious problems and its president, Jacob Zuma, is a highly controversial figure it has become relatively stable, with the continent's largest economy. In certain neighborhoods of Johannesburg today, you can glimpse the possibility of a diverse, peaceful, and creative future. My tour guide couldn't believe how quickly the city was changing. "None of this was here a month ago," he'd say, taking me down a block lined with murals. Then we'd turn a few corners and he'd grin and say, "If you were on this street six months ago, you would have been running."

That is how fast the fires of development are spreading in Johannesburg. One day, a block is Beirut circa 1982. The next, it's TriBeCa 2003.

One of the latest additions to Maboneng is a high-end hotel. I had the good fortune to spend five nights there. Called the Hallmark House, it is 16 stories of coal-black paint and slashing steel beams designed by the Ghanaian-British architect David Adjaye, who has an apartment in the building. It opened in January. I arrived in July. When I told people Joburgers that I was staying in a luxury hotel on Sivewright Avenue between Error and Charles, it blew their minds. They found it unfathomable that someone had opened an upscale hotel on that street.

Johannesburg, South Africa

It was in the Hallmark's gleaming lobby that I met Gerald Garner, who gave me an introduction to the city's dark and fascinating history. Like so many of the people I encountered in Joburg, Garner was a man of many hustles: tour guide, author of two local guidebooks, owner of a tapas bar in a former garage. Together, we set out through Maboneng on foot. The walls passed in a colorful blur of street art. I saw a surreal dreamscape involving a giant diamond balanced on top of a human skull, a towering replica of a famous black-and-white photograph of Nelson Mandela, and a menagerie of African animals zebras, crocodiles, elephants, rhinos. There was also a roaring tiger, which has nothing to do with Africa but looked fantastic.

Johannesburg is the largest city in South Africa. The nearly 8 million residents in its greater metropolitan area include many immigrants and people of European or Asian ancestry, but most of the population is black. For this reason, people often say that Joburg is a "real African city," as distinct from "European" Cape Town, where a greater percentage of the population is white.

After walking a few more blocks, Garner and I boarded a bus headed for the downtown business district, where a handful of new restaurants and residential developments are attracting members of South Africa's growing middle class. As we got off the bus, Garner explained how the city became notorious for crime and poverty   "Detroit times ten," as he helpfully framed it for my American ears.

In Joburg, as in so many cities with industrial pasts, the downtown core is surrounded by rusted-out factory neighborhoods, which in turn are ringed by wealthy suburbs. In the days of apartheid, Garner explained, laws were passed to keep black people out of the inner city, forcing them to live on the outskirts in squalid, crowded settlements called townships. In the 1950s, the apartheid government passed a law stating that no business in Johannesburg could employ more than six black workers. Outside the city, however, the white captains of industry could avail themselves of as much cheap black labor as they pleased. "And so the factories left Johannesburg," Garner said. "The buildings emptied out. Maboneng is a prime example of a place where that happened."

A visitor could spend days touring places associated with the battle against apartheid, beginning with the superb Apartheid Museum. There's also Constitution Hill, the old fort where political prisoners were held, which now houses the country's Constitutional Court and a gallery displaying works by contemporary South African artists. And Nelson Mandela's old law office inside

Chancellor House, the former headquarters of the African National Congress. And Soweto, the largest township in South Africa, which gained international attention in 1976 when police opened fire on a crowd of protesting schoolchildren, killing several and sparking a riot in which hundreds died.

There's a duality to life in South Africa right now that makes it an interesting place to get into conversations with strangers. As I wandered around Johannesburg, I kept thinking of something Garner had said: "In some ways we are a traumatized society. But there is a new generation that is trying to reinvent society, and they want to talk about it."

Jonathan Freemantle, a Cape Town–born painter who came to Johannesburg to make art, is someone who wants to talk about it. "In a way, northern Europe is running out of ideas. It's looking backward," he said. "This place is too young for that. There's a creative revival happening that gives the area a profoundly exciting edge." Three years ago, Freemantle was walking past the defunct Cosmopolitan Hotel, a Victorian building in Maboneng with peeling columns and bricked-up windows, when he realized it could be a great place to have a gallery. Luckily, he had a friend with access to large amounts of capital.

So they bought the building, renovated it, and invited their favorite local artists to hang their work on the walls. Then they asked some of those artists to move their studios into the former guest rooms. They reopened the hotel bar and planted the garden with hydrangeas and roses. The old building, Freemantle told me when I visited, "was like a dowager who was here in the gold rush, and all her snooty friends got scared and fled for the suburbs, and she stayed in her chair with her Versace dress and her G&T. I said, 'Let's pour her a fresh drink and find some young chaps to flirt with her.' We wanted to make this a place where the genteel would mix with the reprobates and artists."

Across the street from the Cosmopolitan, I came across a tiny store named Afrosynth Records. I spent two hours there, hoping to find some of the gorgeous *marabi* jazz that was one of several South African styles Paul Simon borrowed from on his 1986 album *Graceland.* The owner, DJ Okapi, steered me toward a section devoted to another genre: bubblegum, a kind of synth-happy South African disco that emerged in the 1980s.

Most of the labels that produced bubblegum shut down long ago, and South Africa's isolation under

Johannesburg, South Africa

apartheid was one of the reasons the records never reached the rest of the world. As a result, they're very rare, and a kind of cult has grown up around them. As I was leaving the store, a kid with shaggy blond hair caught sight of one of the records I'd pulled off the shelf and asked begged me to give it to him. When I said yes, he clasped his hands together and gave me a little bow.

People say Johannesburg owes its existence to an accident. As the story goes, 130 years ago an English prospector was walking through a barren field in the middle of nowhere when he stubbed his toe. Looking down, he saw he'd stumbled onto a kind of rock that is often found near gold deposits. Within a few years, a city had sprung up on the veld a bustling frontier town of Brits and Australians and failed California 49ers chasing one last chance to make a fortune. Over time, the city reinvented itself again and again, growing first into the biggest and most prosperous city in Africa, then getting razed and rebuilt and surgically segregated by the architects of apartheid, then falling into violent disarray as apartheid collapsed and businesses fled. But it somehow remained a prospector's town a beacon for people from southern Africa and beyond, who came in hopes of realizing their dreams of a better life.

One of those people was the barista who poured me a cup of Ethiopian Kana through a complicated glass contraption at Craft Coffee in Newtown, a neighborhood not far from Maboneng that is beginning to become the kind of place where baristas pour Ethiopian Kana through complicated glass contraptions. He told me his name was Lovejoy that's it, just Lovejoy and when I asked how he became a barista, he paused and said, "It's quite an interesting story."

Johannesburg, South Africa

In 2009, the economy in his native Zimbabwe got so bad that the government stopped printing money. So he hitchhiked to Cape Town, a three-night journey, and got a job sweeping floors at a high-end roastery called Origin Coffee. "After some time I got an opportunity to stand behind the bar pouring coffee, and that was the biggest break I could ever have," he said. A year later, he entered his first barista competition. Two years after that, he was crowned the all-Africa champion. When Craft opened in Johannesburg, the owners tapped him to manage the shop. I asked if he could tell me something about the coffee I was drinking. He said, "You get a lot of dried fig, citrus fruit. They dry the coffee with the skin on, so you get all those good sugars."

Over those first few days, as I ate marjoram-cured lamb-rib *kushiyaki* at Urbanologi, a restaurant in what used to be a warehouse for mining equipment, or listened to that effervescent *marabi* music in the jazz club in the basement of Hallmark House, I kept hearing about a developer named Jonathan Liebmann. People said he had single-handedly willed Maboneng into existence. Articles described him as a "visionary." The more I heard and read, the more curious I became. He seemed to loom over the neighborhood like a colossus.

One day, as I was leaving the hotel, I spotted a guy in his mid 30s waiting for the elevator. He had on the international cool-guy uniform of tight black jeans and leather jacket, and his hair was tied back in a ponytail. It took me a moment to realize I'd seen his picture in some of the articles I'd been reading about Maboneng. "Liebmann?" I called out. I went over and introduced myself, and he invited me to come up with him to the Hallmark's unfinished two-level penthouse, which a team of

Johannesburg, South Africa

workers was racing to complete for him and his pregnant wife before the baby arrived.

Liebmann is the founder of Propertuity, the company responsible for the development of almost every building in Maboneng. Ten years ago, when he was only 24, he bought a sooty brick warehouse at the heart of the area and turned it into Arts on Main, a mix of restaurants, galleries, artists' workshops, and retail spaces. He convinced South African art star William Kentridge to move his private studio into the building, a major coup. Rather than depend on the city's notoriously unreliable police department, he hired his own small army of security guards to keep watch over the streets.

Backed by a silent partner, Liebmann then developed Main Street Life, a building with 178 apartments, a small hotel, and a cinema that specializes in South African independent films. Next came Main Change, which has a co-working space for start-ups and freelancers, a rooftop bar, and a popular Asian-fusion restaurant called the Blackanese. Altogether, Propertuity has developed 30 buildings in the Maboneng neighborhood.

If you met Liebmann, you might observe that he suffers from neither an overabundance of modesty nor a lack of ambition. When I asked about his plans for Maboneng, he said, "I created this neighborhood. It's become so inextricably linked to my identity that I can't imagine ever stopping."

I doubt that Joburg ever looks more deserving of its reputation as a city of opportunity than it does from the penthouse of a Propertuity high-rise. Of course, not all Joburgers see the city this way. At a backyard barbecue I met Anaz Mia, one of the founders of a printmaking collective whose work calls attention to issues of racial and economic injustice, and his wife, a constitutional lawyer named Alex Fitzgerald. The three of us hit it off and quickly got into a conversation about gentrification. Mia spent a good hour laying out a detailed critique of the changes afoot in Joburg. "And yet," he said at the end, "I have to admit that there's something magical about being able to walk down the street with Alex without fear of getting robbed."

The collective that Mia belongs to is called Danger Gevaar Ingozi. The day after the barbecue, I stopped by their studio on the outskirts of Maboneng, where the artists showed me their black-and-white lino-cut prints. Linocut printing, a technique in which artists cut into blocks of linoleum with chisels, has a proud history in Johannesburg. Under apartheid, black artists relied on the medium to create the iconic posters and pamphlets of the resistance, and artists at DGI see themselves as heirs to that tradition.

One of their starkest images took its inspiration from Maboneng itself. Two years ago, when developers evicted people from a building in the area, protesters marched through the streets, burning tires and throwing rocks until the police drove them away with rubber bullets. In the rebellious spirit of the apartheid-era printers, the DGI artists took up their chisels in solidarity. The resulting print depicts a group of black protesters being forcibly removed from the hallway of a men's hostel that was being repurposed by developers. It is a testament to both the complexities and the possibilities of Maboneng that you can see a copy of the piece on display in a Maboneng wine bar, upstairs from a truck that sells frozen yogurt and goji-berry iced tea.

Johannesburg, South Africa

On my last night in Joburg, I accompanied Mia and Fitzgerald and some of their friends to an art opening at August House, a loft building a couple blocks from Maboneng. "This is the avant-garde," Mia said as we walked into the space. About a hundred people were standing around, chatting over an electronic dance track and drinking beer. Someone was cooking chicken on an indoor grill. Everyone was wearing something fun a fluorescent-yellow Adidas jumpsuit stands out in my memory.

At the far end of the room, I stopped in front of a mixed-media piece depicting a group of men sitting around a boom box, most of them dressed in the style of 1960s Hollywood. One wore boots that resembled spats. Another had on a mauve suit and black gloves, with a cream homburg balanced on his knee. The style of the image was sketchlike yet fully realized, as though the artist had first rendered the scene completely, then erased all the details that didn't matter. I tracked down its creator, Bambo Sibiya, and told him that I loved his work.

Like the men in the painting, Sibiya was dressed impeccably, in a tailored suit of royal blue with a shirt and tie of the same rich color. He told me that he'd based the figures on people like his uncles, who came to Johannesburg in the 1960s to work in the mines. "They used music and fashion as their way of fighting back against the oppression of apartheid," he said. "They used the power of being gentlemen." Several of his other paintings were hanging on the walls. They captured similar scenes, all in the same distinctive style.

Bambo Sibiya look out for that name. I believe he has a bright future. He's retrieving moments from Johannesburg's dark past and turning them into scenes of vibrant beauty and light. I can't think of anyone who better embodies the spirit of the city.

Going to Johannesburg for the first time

Cape Town, Kruger National Park, KwaZulu-Natal: South Africa has some big-hitting sights. But a lot of visitors leave the country's largest city, Johannesburg, off their itineraries.

This is a mistake: it's the best place to learn about South Africa's past and look to its future. And if you need a break from the city's size and energy, you can head off for nearby safaris, adventure sports and glimpses into the history of humanity.

Whether it's your first visit to South Africa or your 50th, you should make time to feel the Jozi vibes here are a few tips on getting the most out of it

Why should I go?

Johannesburg is South Africa's most diverse, progressive and energetic city, the country's best showcase for activism and optimism. There's really nowhere better if you want to see the face of modern South Africa, and get a sense of how far the nation's come and where it's going next.

Though the city like the rest of South Africa is still dealing with the legacy of racial segregation, it has become a truly diverse place. Walk around Johannesburg and you'll hear snatches of Afrikaans, Zulu and Xhosa, but you may also catch some Urdu, Hindi or Chinese.

High-intensity in everything it does, Johannesburg manages not only to be the country's biggest and the continent's richest city but also at least according to the locals the world's largest man-made forest. There are some ten million trees dotted around, lending the place a surprisingly fresh and spacious feel.

But is it safe to visit Johannesburg?

The short answer is: yes, it's safe to visit.

The slightly longer answer is that some areas are safer than others. The northern suburbs are fine to wander around freely, and downtown areas like Maboneng a no-go area barely a decade ago have become safe and exciting models of urban regeneration.

Tourists are most at risk of opportunistic crimes like theft and mugging. The best way to protect yourself is to use your common sense: don't stand on a street corner with your DSLR around your neck staring at a map; don't carry all your cash around with you; and if you're going to a less safe district, hire a local guide.

Great! So what should I do in the day?

As you'd expect from a city this size, there's a lot to do starting with retail therapy. Other than Melville's 27 Boxes, a bunch of shipping containers filled with shops and restaurants, the northern suburbs are mostly home to opulent, anonymous malls. Downtown is much more inspiring, with Maboneng's Market on Main a Sunday staple for arts, crafts and street food and Collector's Treasury a labyrinthine, longstanding bookshop among the best spots.

To get to grips with Johannesburg, try one of the excellent tours on offer. On Mainstreetwalks' Maboneng Precinct tour, for instance, you'll discover the best of this exciting district's community-led regeneration. To find out more about the stunning graffiti you'll spot on your walk, book onto one of Past Experiences' street art tours. And to learn about Soweto, try Lebo's tuk-tuk tours. The entertaining, knowledgeable local guides will show you both the township's struggles and its hopes for the future.

The city's museums include MOAD, the continent's first museum dedicated to design, and Newtown's cavernous MuseuMAfricA, with thoughtful exhibits on Johannesburg's art and history.

Further from the centre, the Apartheid Museum is a nuanced exploration of the history and legacy of racial segregation in South Africa, which is also the focus at the Mandela House Museum and Hector Pieterson Memorial and Museum in Soweto.

And in the evening?
Start your Friday or Saturday night in Fordsburg, the historic Indian district, and hit up the night market around Mint Street. Arrive hungry, as you won't be able to resist just one samosa, a tiny bite of *uttappam*, a couple of *jalebi*...

If you're still (somehow) hungry, head next to Maboneng for memorable African-Asian fusion at Blackanese, a generous Argentine grill at Che, or Ethiopian cuisine at Little Addis Cafe. After dinner join the young, mixed crowd at Living Room for a sundowner with a view.

Continue your night by exploring Joburg's thriving jazz scene Braamfontein institution The Orbit is known as South Africa's best jazz bar, with Sophiatown's Afrikan Freedom Station another historic venue. A more recent addition is the Marabi Club, which pays homage to the early 20th-century marabi music scene; the classic cocktails and waistcoated waiters set the vintage vibe.

Where should I stay?
The northern suburbs offer luxury hotels and prestigious developments, with Sandton the best known but its international hotel chains and mega-

malls could be anywhere. Melville and Parkhurst are less polished, more endearing options with good streetlife and independent businesses; consider Little Forest Guest House and Die Agterplaas.

In the CBD (Central Business District), you could spoil yourself with a stay at the new Hallmark House hotel, in an arresting industrial-style building just outside Maboneng. An excellent budget option is Curiocity Backpackers, right in the heart of the district.

Alternatively, head to Soweto and stay at Lebo's Soweto Backpackers, run by local Lebo Malepa. This sprawling township about a third of Joburgers live here is where the city's non-white residents were forced to live during apartheid. Its history is one of struggle but also of hope, encapsulated by

Vilakazi Street, where you can see the homes of both Nelson Mandela and Desmond Tutu.

And what if I want to escape the city for a while?
There are plenty of places nearby to get some breathing space, with the Magaliesberg mountain range particularly popular with Joburgers head to Hartbeespoort Dam to get a cable car straight up into the mountains. Relax afterwards at Silver Orange Bistro, with its contemporary South African cuisine, wine list long enough for repeat visits, and gorgeous setting in an orange orchard.

If you're after adrenaline rather than R&R, try Ama Zwing Zwing, a great zipline experience under an hour's drive from the city; the larger Canopy Tour Magaliesberg is about an hour and a half. For hiking and biking, make a beeline for the forty square kilometres of Kgaswane Mountain Reserve. You can camp overnight and follow the Rustenberg

Hiking Trail for a couple of days, or explore one of the shorter routes.

The archeological sites of the Cradle of Humankind are easily accessible from Joburg; the Sterkfontein Caves, where Mrs Ples and Little Foot (australopithecus fossils) were found, are a highlight. At the Maropeng Museum you can see the incredible homo naledi fossils excavated in the area plus a fascinating video about their discovery in a tiny chamber almost 100 feet underground (claustrophobes should cover their eyes).

Going on safari in the malaria-free reserves of North West Province is another great way to escape the city. Madikwe is an excellent reserve near the Botswana border, and is refreshingly uncrowded as no independent day visits are allowed (you have to book through one of the lodges).

To safari independently you should head to Pilanesberg, just a couple of hours' drive from Joburg. That said, you'll still get the most memorable experience by staying at a lodge Kwa Maritane and Bakubung are great choices for their experienced rangers who will impress you with their knowledge on a game drive or bush walk.

Things to Know ahead ofgoing to Johannesburg

<u>Get out of the airport</u>. As a Johannesburg native, my blood pumps with a loathing for Cape Town, the way a serious East Coaster might feel about the West Coast of the U.S. (or vice versa.) That might sound bitter, but you would be too if you had to constantly convince people that your city is worth more than a two-hour layover at O.R. Tambo Airport on the way to the promised land of Table Mountain, two oceans, and

hypergentrification. Cape Town is pretty, I'll admit it. But only grudgingly. Now, about that crime rep: South Africa is notorious for the frequency and variety of crime, from street muggings to bank heists. I wish I could say it was overblown but we do have a problem. The fact is, though, that Johannesburg's province of Gauteng has a much lower crime rate than the Western Cape. So cancel that connecting flight, baby; you know it's Joburg you really want. Grab a ticket on the Gautrain, our luxury transit railway system, and for God's sake don't get off at Sandton.

<u>Seriously, skip Sandton.</u> Many visitors who dare to venture out of the airport are directed to Sandton, the new commercial and business center of the city. That means malls. Malls and banks. It's shiny, sanitized, and expensive and they say it's safe. It's basically an extension of the airport.

<u>Start with a walk in Rosebank</u>. One stop beyond Sandton on the Gautrain from the airport, this northern suburb is a cultural middle ground of the city. It's both urban and suburban, quiet but arty, gentrified just enough to feel secure but close enough to the real city to get your feet wet. A walk down Jan Smuts Avenue in Rosebank will include coffee bars, flower shops, vintage stores, and art galleries, like the avant-garde Goodman Gallery, which is plugged into all the latest artistic talent.

<u>Be confident, not cocky</u>. Crime is an undeniable concern for travelers to Johannesburg, but fear shouldn't stop you from experiencing the city. Just follow the basic rules of not flashing your goods and not looking too lost. Don't be afraid to explore, but don't take unnecessary risks. If driving, don't keep valuables in sight of the windows unless you want to experience one of our

famous "smash and grabs." Best keep everything locked up in the trunk.

Drive, then walk. Johannesburg is an expansive and expanding city. During apartheid, it was extended peripherally so the black population could be banished to the outskirts, but still live close enough to come in and work for the whites. Getting around has never been convenient, and at some point you will need vehicular transport. There are private taxis, which have become more visible and accessible since our tourism industry has blossomed, plus taxi apps, the imperfect-but-it's-a-start Rhea Vaya bus transit system, and the informal minibus taxi which the adventurous can hail using one of these hand signals. Or do what many visitors do and just rent a car. But you should only use the wheels to get from place to place, and then get out and walk. (We are murderous drivers though, so please beware of traffic.)

<u>Expect parking tips</u>. When parking your car, don't freak out if you get unsolicited help from one of our car guards. They're kind of informal valets, usually just a guy on the street who has probably never owned a car but will give you expert parallel parking tips. Listen to him, and tip him back. The going rate is at least 10 Rand ($0.80).

<u>Look out for robots</u>. Whether walking or driving, the traffic lights or robots, as we call them are where the action is. Whether the lights flash green, red, or orange, they all mean "stop" because there will be some daredevil on the opposite side trying to make it through before the red light, or during, or after. At traffic lights you will also be accosted by street entrepreneurs, who can come in handy if you really need an in-car phone charger, suit hanger, or pumice stone in a pinch. It wouldn't hurt to support their enterprise, so keep some change up front to buy a newspaper or whatever.

But again, don't unlock your doors or lower your windows too much because the vendors aren't the only ones looking for opportunity.

<u>Dip into Norwood</u>. Like many economically precarious societies, South Africa is roiling with racial and xenophobic tension. Between flare-ups, however, there is tacit coexistence. The communities dissolve into each other and you barely know when you are moving from one quarter to another. Take Grant Avenue in Norwood, the last bastion of the city's old Jewish neighborhood. The most popular restaurant here is The Schwarma Company, which despite its name is most famous for its massive Mediterranean-spiced steaks and ribs. It's run by Palestinian twin brothers. You should go there. But go on the Jewish Sabbath, when you're more likely to get a table. (Also, one of the twins is really friendly while the other one is a total grump. Have fun trying to

figure out which is which.) Further up Grant Ave towards Orange Grove and Yeoville, you will be speaking French with Senegalese, Ivorian, and Congolese Joburgers. If you want to wash that steak down with cheap beer and fresh fish grilled on an outside barbecue, say the magic words "Où se trouve La Camerounaise?" When you get there, ask for Lucy and thank me later. On that note…

<u>Don't look for South African food</u>. It's no use: Johannesburg is too cosmopolitan. Eat your way through this city to know it. Go to Fordsburg for Turkish shawarma at Istanbul café and South Indian fried fish, crab curry, and *masala dosa* from Dosa Hut. Walk a few blocks up to Little Mogadishu and have tea and samosas at Kisimayo. Head to Chinese Northern Foods in Cyrildene for duck with potatoes, jellyfish salad, and their unmissable "Pie Like Hat," a chewy flatbread. Get *piri-piri* prawns the size of your toddler at the

unpretentious Portuguese Troyeville Hotel, which also happens to have some of the best views of the city. These are all part of the South African experience.

<u>Clean up with *carne*</u>. Then, there is perhaps the most South African experience: eating meat at a carwash. In Johannesburg's townships, the militarized apartheid police suppressed large gatherings, from dancing and drinking at *shebeens* to wedding parties and funerals. People had to find imaginative ways to socialize. You can get a sense of that vibe at the E'Socialink *shisa nyama* (the Zulu word for barbecue) carwash in Soweto the township on the south side of Johannesburg, once home to the Mandelas and other great apartheid-struggle veterans. Another great meat-and-entertainment hangout is Joe's Butchery *shisa nyama* in Alexandra township, where the

ubiquitous grilled meat comes with solid live music and DJs on a Sunday night.

Take the plunge in Soweto. If you've got a strong stomach, you might try the tripe at the *shisa nyama*. If you want to test your gut even further, try swinging between the graffiti-covered Orlando Towers. These twin cooling towers of a decommissioned coal-fired power station are Soweto's most distinctive landmarks, and you can bungee-jump off the small bridge between them or into one of the towers if that's your thing. While you're up on the bridge, see if you can spot Nelson Mandela's house on Vilakasi Street. And while you're down in the south of Johannesburg, it'd be criminal of you not to take the 20-minute drive from Soweto to the indelible Apartheid Museum and learn about us.

Johannesburg, South Africa

Catch a movie with the masses. Most people who've been to Cape Town will tell you it doesn't feel like Africa. That's because the local government has managed to build a bubble around its privileged (white) minority. This would be impossible in Joburg, because we all live on top of one another. Right next to gleaming Sandton is Alexandra township, a messy, chaotic stronghold of the hoi polloi. Here you will find Kings Cinema, an art-deco movie house and a popular venue for performances by local musicians like the Alexandra All Star Band and the Jazz Maniacs. Kings was first established in the 1950s, but had to be rebuilt after it was bombed by apartheid forces in 1984.

Go to town. For me, one of the must-go parts of Joburg is the original central business district, known simply as "town." The main street to know here is Commissioner Street, which you should walk from top to bottom. The route will bring you to the hipster Arts on Main district on Fox Street, the formidable Market Theatre, and Museum Africa in Newtown. On your way you will find restaurants, curio stands, barbershops, and most importantly, traces of history. The street is decorated with busts of historically significant Africans, old colonial buildings like the Rand Club the city's oldest private members' club and Marshall Street prison, where my uncle was once detained under apartheid and managed to escape disguised as a woman in a sari. Not to mention the infamous John Vorster Square prison, where too many of our great anti-apartheid stalwarts died in detention.

<u>Say "howzit" a lot</u>. As a greeting or an icebreaker, with strangers or with friends, it's the easiest way to make an entrance or enquire about someone's well-being. This is our go-to word, with which you can sculpt an entire conversation. Behold:

Johannesburg, South Africa

Person A: Howzit?

Person B: All good bro, howzit?

Person A: Yeah man good, howzit going with your business?

Person B: Great. How's your mum doing? Tell her I said howzit.

Person A: Cool I'll pass it on.

<u>Embrace cheap laughs</u>. The seeds of Johannesburg's stand-up comedy scene were planted a decade ago in a few underground clubs frequented by students and stoners. As demonstrated by (but not purely thanks to) Trevor Noah's international success, South African comedy has bloomed to rival more established scenes in New York and London. Johannesburg is home to top international acts like Loyiso Gola, Kagiso Lediga, Loyiso Madinga, and Mojakisane Lehoko, who have not forgotten their roots. They still perform frequently at low-key venues in the

bohemian Melville area and newly-gentrified Braamfontein, where you will find them doing groundbreaking material on Tuesday nights in Kitcheners, a chilled-out bar which turns into club afterwards, with top-notch DJs playing amazing South African house tracks. All this for under two U.S. dollars. Gotta love that exchange rate.

<u>Visit Joburg's "Met"</u>**.** The Johannesburg Art Gallery (JAG) is my city's answer to New York's Metropolitan Museum of Art, complete with an adjacent park. The Met's vicinity to Central Park has nothing on Joubert Park, which can be seen from the JAG and boasts a vibrant population of "*nyaope* boys," young people who have become hopelessly addicted to the street drug, made with rat poison and HIV meds. You're going to have to avoid these kids, but the whole thing is a devastating example of how Joburg refuses to sugarcoat anything. It says a lot that the largest art

gallery on the African continent, an exquisite old building bursting with local and international masterpieces, is nested within one of the country's greatest social failures.

<u>Buy silk and samosas at the Oriental Plaza.</u> Fietas is one of the famous old Johannesburg neighborhoods where many races lived and mixed joyfully until they were segregated under apartheid. Indian families and shops were moved to Lenasia and Fordsburg, where many remain today. In Fordsburg, the government pushed traders into a shopping center called The Oriental Plaza, where you can still buy absolutely anything, from hot samosas to knitting needles and leather goods to Kashmiri furniture and, of course, lots and lots of gold. This place is also known for its endless variety of textiles, and skilled tailors.

<u>Get stuffed</u>. When we talk about Indian food, it's usually an umbrella term for the South Asian delicacies available at the countless Bengali, Pakistani, and Indian restaurants in Fordsburg. But then there is South African Indian food which is rather less sophisticated, but wholly satisfying. If you want to know the epitome of comfort food, chow down on one of the specials at the iconic Solly's Corner, an institution run by a sublime dynasty whose sons have spent generation after generation serving hot vinegar-sodden chips (known as *slaap* chips), sausages, steak, salad, and kebabs known as *frikkadels*, all stuffed generously into a sandwich that will always taste the same. There are so few things we can rely on in this world. Start and end your Joburg sojourn at Solly's Corner for something to count on.

Johannesburg, South Africa

Johannesburg diversity shaping Environment and Lifestyle

Joburg is the one your mother warned you about. She's pierced, tattooed, laughs too loud, and drinks and smokes too much. While most cities seduce you with their subtle charms, Jozi just knocks you on the head and drags you in. After two holidays in South Africa, I decided to pack up my life in suburban Atlanta and move to Cape Town. I had only planned to pass through Johannesburg on my way south, but 21 years later I'm still here. Jozi must have slipped something into my drink when I wasn't looking. How else could I have fallen for an ill-tempered wild child with such a bad reputation? But love her I do. And I'm not alone. Millions from around the world have fallen under her spell, all the way back to the city's founding in 1886.

Joburg was born from a sudden lust for gold, entirely unplanned and hundreds of miles from any viable water source. For beneath her lie the world's largest gold reserves, a 300km arc producing more than 40,000 tons (1.5-billion ounces) of bling - accounting for nearly half the gold ever mined on earth.

Thousands of thrill-seekers, fortune-hunters, swindlers, merchants, bureaucrats, clergymen and prostitutes came to coo over her golden cradle. Unlike in other New World cities, left to develop unique traits over centuries, every member of Joburg's somewhat dysfunctional family - including her ruling class and underclass, criminals and police, as well as her Christian, Jewish, Muslim and agnostic aunts and uncles - arrived on the same day.

Johannesburg, South Africa

As an instant city, Johannesburg has always been a place of immigrants. Being half-Italian and half-Croatian, I fit in perfectly. In the northern suburbs the first-generation immigrant stock among whites - Greek, Jewish, Italian, Portuguese, Lebanese - easily outnumber Dutch- and German-descended Afrikaners. And the dawn of democracy in South Africa in 1994, combined with the Yugoslav civil war and the fall of the Berlin Wall, created a second-generation influx of Eastern Europeans, as well as Chinese, Bangladeshis, Pakistanis and Thais, not to mention other Africans. It's a mix that's unique on the continent. Almost overnight, a new Chinatown has taken root in the previously Jewish suburb of Cyrildene; and the high street of what has traditionally been Joburg's Little Italy, Orange Grove, has become Little Nigeria.

The full spectrum of the city's ethnic and religious diversity can be experienced by driving north along the M1 motorway. At the crest of the ridge leading into the suburban basin, the six spires of the temple of the Church of Jesus Christ of Latter-day Saints appear on the right, followed by the Houghton Masjid, St Jerome's Croatian Catholic church, the Greek Orthodox Christian church of the Pantanassa, the Great Park synagogue, the Lebanese Maronite Catholic church, St Sergius Russian Orthodox church and the Nizamiye Turkish Masjid - all in a 15-minute drive.

If there was little planning involved in Joburg's birth, even less was applied to her development. Pathways between shanties became horse trails before becoming roads, then motorways. Town planning was in place, but practical micro logic always prevailed over a macro grand master plan. 'Johannesburg's city centre has been rebuilt four times in less than a century,' says 33-year-old Joburg-born architect and dapper man-about-town

Johannesburg, South Africa

Brian McKechnie who, while still based in the suburbs, has snapped up a city-centre apartment in the historic Ansteys Building, keeping a firm eye on the future. 'The first round of development was tin shacks and tents, followed by the Transvaal Republic vernacular, then the British Empire style and, later, Art Deco. The last - the post-war skyscraper boom - still stands, and we're now left with a very well-preserved 1970s-era city centre, which is unique.

The city developed like an onion, quickly expanding outwards in all directions, ring by ring. They say 10 years in Joburg is like a half-century in other cities. Previously fashionable suburbs have simply been discarded like abandoned outfits on a teen's date night. With each passing decade the expansion continued, and now the area contained within its city limits is larger than that of Los Angeles, although the sprawl, which might otherwise seem overwhelming, is softened by dozens of village-like suburbs centered on high streets.

This place has a decidedly American vibe. But again, rather than reading her script, Jozi has improvised, developing a New York brain and a Los Angeles body. So while the shiny-new California-style sprawl is in place - shopping malls, housing estates, townships and office parks, complete with palm trees, all connected by impressive new motorways and rapid rail systems - there's also a tangible coating of rust-belt grittiness that permeates the city.

Until very recently, that grittiness was particularly noticeable around Joburg's inner-city core, where property prices had plummeted after big businesses moved out to the northern suburbs. 'Rock bottom came around the year 2000,' says

Sharon Lewis of the Johannesburg Development Agency. 'From that point onwards, it became official policy to intervene and upgrade the infrastructure while brokering strategic property deals.' As a result, the agency developed new icons for the city, including the Nelson Mandela Bridge (completed in 2003), Constitution Hill and Newtown (from 2001 onwards), paving the way for private developers to reinvest

The nip-and-tuck approach is working. Forward-thinking young property developers saw promising gaps in the abandoned city centre. Jonathan Liebmann created Maboneng, a hip live-work-play district carved out of the industrial eastern fringe; and Adam Levy began the redevelopment of the Braamfontein district. Galleries, cafés, one-off retailers, studios and restaurants have all sprung up, seemingly overnight. Joburgers are notoriously cynical, but even its hardest-to-impress citizens are taking note.

Researching a story on the city centre's regeneration in 2010, I met the team behind South Point, a property-development company whose core business is providing housing to nearly 5,000 university students in revamped 1950s office blocks. I found myself infected by the urban-regeneration bug. A few months later I joined the company, still creating stories - but now out of bricks and mortar. And it's a fast-paced tale: in 2010 there were only one or two places to buy a cappuccino in Braamfontein; now there are seven independent coffee bars, including two roasteries, in just one block, all doing a roaring trade as international government organisations, creative industries and retailers increasingly return to the area.

Johannesburg, South Africa

For the first time since the city's founding, Joburgers are beginning to reinhabit places they've previously abandoned, seeking relief from what the city's creative class calls 'mall fatigue'. Says McKechnie, 'Anyone younger than 40 who grew up in suburban Joburg has probably grown up in a shopping mall. Joburg was always a car-based city, but there's an entire generation who've never crossed a four-lane street on foot and don't know how to parallel park. Back in the 1970s, the first mega-malls might have been new and interesting to our parents. That was such a turbulent time in South Africa, I think they sought a sense of order and comfort in the malls. Not so for us. There's such a blandness and sameness about them. In the northern suburbs you'll find a lot of architecture driven by fake history and reality-aversion, places that are meant to make you feel like you're in Old World Europe, when in fact they've only been there six months. Younger, more forward-looking people are starting to appreciate the city centre, seeking out authentic experiences, architecture and neighbourhoods.'

Now suburbanites flock to inner-city food markets in their thousands every weekend - on Saturdays to Braamfontein's Neighbourgoods Market, on Sundays to Market On Main in Maboneng. For many young Joburgers these markets have provided their first taste of street life without climate control. The pace of change is mind-boggling. The first wave, driven by pierced and tattooed youth culture, was quickly followed by a second wave of fashion-forward parents pushing babies in Italian prams, who are now supplemented by camera-swinging, small-town and fringe-suburb visitors riding the third wave. Trendoids and grannies sit side by side tucking into Jewish nosh at Maboneng's Eat Your Heart Out café, under an oversized map of Johannesburg with the street names reimagined in Hebrew. On the other side of town, in Braamfontein, Puma launched its South African flagship two years ago - the first international brand to open a stand-alone store on a Joburg city-centre street - and was quickly followed by the flagship premises of Virgin Mobile and the L'Oréal Institute, with more big names set to follow.

The city's cultural scene is also exploding, with the rise of annual events involving previously marginalised communities: Chinese New Year and Diwali, for instance, and the Portuguese Lusito Land festival. 'We're entering a period of cultural reawakening,' says Neil Dundas of the groundbreaking Goodman Gallery, which represents an impressive stable of internationally collectable contemporary South African artists such as William Kentridge, David Goldblatt, Kendell Geers, Mikhael

Subotzky, Sam Nhlengethwa and David Koloane. 'The city's established cultural calendar is being reinvented and new cultural arenas are opening up, like the annual Joburg Art Fair, which has grown tremendously.

The photographic exhibition *Rise and Fall of Apartheid* at Museum Africa last year was co-curated by Okwui Enwezor (who's also the curator of this year's VeniceBiennale and the first African-born person to take on that role in the art event's 100-year history). More than a thousand people attended the opening night party, which was hosted in the streets before moving into the museum - something that would have been unthinkable even two or three years back. The Wits Art Museum is the new face on the block, known for its collection of contemporary South African art, and home to the most important collection of traditional sub-equatorial African art on the continent.'

Chilean-born gallery owner Ricardo Fornoni moved to Johannesburg from London in 2004, opening the Res Gallery in the leafy northern suburb of Parkwood three years later. 'It was a very disparate art scene, controlled by a handful of galleries, when I first arrived,' he says. 'Since then there's been a renaissance of sorts, with all these little galleries popping up everywhere. Now you can find 20 in a relatively small area. The market itself is still quite small, but it's growing as the smaller spaces seem to have made the scene more accessible to a younger crowd, and there's a lot more action taking place.'

Joburg has always had a lively theatre scene, dating back to the long-defunct Theatre Royal, which opened shortly after the city's founding. The past decade has seen new theatres opening, including the Teatro at Montecasino and The Lyric, and the reopening of the Alexander Theatre, rounding out the mix of dozens of performance spaces and theatre complexes. The state-of-the-art Soweto Theatre opened in Jabulani two years ago, adding another 420 seats to the city's estimated tally of about 17,000, and the historic Market Theatre in Newtown is getting a £6million refit.

When I first arrived in 1992, I'd hang out in Rosebank, a compact and tree-lined suburb known for its galleries, interiors shops and restaurants. It was home to Cranks, Joburg's only Thai restaurant; Cinema Nouveau, the city's only venue dedicated to art films; and the Brazilian, a coffee bar famed for its conveyer-belt delivery of cappuccinos. If I walked into the Brazilian on any given Thursday night I would bump into a dozen mates. Now I am hard-pressed to bump into anyone I know more

Johannesburg, South Africa

than once or twice a year, as restaurants and bars are appearing in dozens of instant suburbs that never existed in the early 1990s. The rebirth of the inner city has countered this, providing a centralised, human-scaled touch point for Joburg - where Sandton, quite literally, meets Soweto, and often for the first time.

Another new area where people are connecting is the charity fundraising circuit, where Joburgers give the Big Rich Texas girls a run for their money. Joburg is unique on the African continent in that it's a self-funding city, with philanthropy running through its veins. Giving back is part of its psyche. There's a fundraiser almost every night, bringing in cash for organisations concerned with an exhaustive list of societal issues - children and gender, environment and wildlife, arts and culture, education and health. A recent Monday-night launch for a Dutch-driven HIV initiative, Orange

Babies South Africa, saw the 79-year-old Zimbabwean jazz legend Dorothy Masuka share the stage with 36-year-old Brussels-born Afrikaans rock queen Karen Zoid. The full spectrum of Joburg's air-kiss brigade - fashion, big business, sport, theatre - turned out in full force, partying until 1am.

'Work is work and play time is play time, and we play very well,' says Tselane Tambo, daughter of anti-apartheid icons Oliver and Adelaide Tambo. She moved to Johannesburg from London, and now works as a fundraiser for the Adelaide Tambo School for disabled children in White City, Soweto. 'When I first arrived, I found it a lot slower than London. I found it quiet. But now, although it still feels suburban, it's suburbia with an adrenalin rush.'

Johannesburg, South Africa

The Cultural Scene Is Exploding, With The Rise of Events Involving Previously Marginalised Groups

Since coming to Johannesburg 20 years ago, 36-year-old Bulgarian-born filmmaker and actor Stanimir Stoykov has pumped out eight films, with a ninth in production. Like Baltimore's John Waters and Madrid's Pedro Almodóvar in their early days, Stoykov self-funds, cajoling a potent mix of celebrities and underground drag queens into working for free. Joburg has always served as the bad-girl backdrop for his below-the-radar films, including *Lesbian Braai*, *Me Kutch Ne Karongi (I Don't Mind)* and *Fanny*. 'Joburg is integral to my work, and there's a lot of talent here,' says Stoykov. 'It's a rebel town. I shoot everywhere without permits. We even shot a scene at the airport, where we had an actor impersonating Britney Spears arriving in South Africa. And we just shot it, with a biiiiiig camera! You can imagine. But no one blinked an eye.'

'Joburg is the cultural heart of South Africa,' says Tamara Dey, lead singer of dance band Flash Republic, who also stars in Stoykov's latest film, *Spotlight Terror*, about a pop star who kills her competition. 'Young people are flocking back to the inner city, fearlessly. It's full of possibilities if you're creative, free-spirited and adventurous. Joburg's got a lot of heart, with a non-stop clash of cultures and energy - and young people are tapping into it. Joburg is the future.'

Indispensable places to visit in Johannesburg

Constitution Hill
The ramparts that surround the hilltop in central Johannesburg once contained a feared prison that held Mohatma Gandhi and Nelson Mandela

(though not, of course, at the same time). After the end of apartheid, the notorious site was transformed into the highest court in the land.

The old cells became a museum, and the ramparts a walkway overlooking the skyline. Outside the chambers of the Constitutional Court, artwork lines the corridors, interpreting the freedoms enshrined in South Africa's Bill of Rights.

Lebo's Soweto Backpackers
Lebo's backpacker accommodaton in Orlando West that also offers walking, bicycle and tuk-tuk tours

Lebo's is so much more than just a hostel. Located in Orlando West, the most-visited neighborhood in Soweto, it's a charming place to stay and has become a center for exploring the streets of the township.

The backpackers organizes tours by bicycle and by tuk-tuk that take in the tourist highlights, but also in workers' hostels, churches and community centers that give a sense of the rhythm of life.

Founder Lebo and his family have transformed an open field across the street from their home into a a visitor's center and restaurant that serves up homestyle cooking, including bunny chows (curry in a bread loaf), potjies (cauldrons of stew) and of course a braai.

Lebo's Soweto Backpackers, 10823A Pooe Street, Orlando West Soweto; +27 11 936 3444

Brunch at the Westcliff
This luxury hotel rises over a hillside in a part of town that was built as the residential playground for the city's gold rush mining barons.

The Westcliff was recently bought by the Four Seasons, which painted over its trademark pink walls in favor of more muted shades of grey. The restaurants and their menus have been given a modern facelift, but still serve decadent meals with views over the city's northern suburbs. On a good day, diners can see the elephants roaming in their pens at the nearby zoo.

Four Seasons Hotel The Westcliff, 67 Jan Smuts Avenue, Saxonwold 2132, Johannesburg; +27 (0)11 481 6000

Dinner at the Saxon Hotel

Top South African chef Luke Dale-Roberts has set up a restaurant at the Saxon Hotel, one of the city's toniest hideaways favored by visiting celebs who like to ensconce themselves in the compounds vast gardens. It's hard to find a more beautiful spot for a sundowner, followed by an unrivaled tasting menu at Luke Dale-Roberts at the Saxon (guests take a small, private elevator up to the dining room). The wine pairings are as exquisite as the food.

The Saxon, 36 Saxon Road, Sandhurst 2196, Johannesburg; +27 (0) 11 292 6000

Vilakazi Street
This two-lane road in Soweto connects the residences of two South African luminaries: Nelson Mandela and Archbishop Desmond Tutu.

That makes it the only street in the world that's been home to two Nobel Peace Prize winners. Mandela's house, where he returned after his release from prison, is now a small museum holding intimate mementos of his family life. Tutu's is still a private residence.

Visiting the museum doesn't take long, but it's impossible to see Soweto without stopping at its most iconic addresses.

Other homes along the road have been transformed into restaurants, from homestyle buffets to a swanky wine bar.

Hector Pieterson Memorial

A short walk from the upper end of Vilakazi Street, the Hector Pieterson Memorial remembers the most famous victim of the 1976 uprising in Soweto, when a peaceful student protest demanding better education was crushed by apartheid police.

Hector Pieterson was 13 when he was shot dead and the photo of his body being carried away became an iconic image of the student protests.

The memorial explains what life was like in the township during the dark days of the past, in simple but powerful exhibits. Its gift shop also carries an excellent selection of books on South African history.

Apartheid Museum

Yes, the museum is a searing look at the devastation that apartheid wrought on South African society, but it's also a much broader look at the country's more distant history as well, delving into the conditions that allowed apartheid to emerge.

From the entrance, visitors are invited to put themselves into experience of violent racial segregation, forcing everyone to choose a race as they enter through separate doors.

A room of limp hangman's nooses pays homage to victims of the state's executions. Audio and video records bring to life the memories of that era, a past so recent that some of the people featured are still alive.

Apartheid Museum, Northern Park Way and Gold Reef Rd, Johannesburg

Johannesburg, South Africa

Neighbourgoods Market in Braamfontein
Every Saturday in a parking garage in Braamfontein, foodies gather around giant paellas, raw oysters, and lots of craft beers.

The Neighbourgoods Market fills two floors with innovative foods from across the city, drawing in students from nearby universities and urban explorers from farther afield.

The market has helped drive the redevelopment in Braamfontein, a neighborhood with a long history as a bohemian and student enclave.

The Neighborgoods Market Johannesburg, 73 Juta Street, Braamfontein, Johannesburg

Wits Art Museum
The University of the Witwatersrand, known widely as Wits and pronounced "Vits" in the Afrikaans way, recently remodeled its art museum

with floor-to-ceiling windows that open its displays to the street.

The museum holds a significant collection by African artists, but also hosts international exhibitions, including a major show of Andy Warhol screen prints. Entrance is free, and the museum's cafe serves one of the most affordable and tastiest lunches in town.

Wits Art Museum, University Corner, Jorissen St & Bertha St, Johannesburg 2050; +27 11 717 1365

Market Theatre
The theater was founded in 1976, at the height of the struggle against apartheid, in what was once a fruit market. Through an unusual snag in apartheid's web of regulations, it was allowed to employ mixed-race casts, and quickly became known as the "theater of the Struggle."

Now its stages host revivals of struggle classics, while promoting new work as well. Famous actors still frequent the theater, both on stage and in audiences.

Market also recently finished a painstaking renovation of the Windybrow Theatre, which is based in a Victorian home from the gold rush era that's now a landmark in the rough neighborhood of Hillbrow.

The Market Theatre, 56 Margaret Mcingana St, Newtown, Johannesburg; +27 (0)11 832 1641

Carlton Tower viewing deck
The tallest building in Africa, Carlton Tower has a 50th floor viewing deck that shows the sweep of the city, from what's left of the gold rush mine dumps (most have been re-mined into oblivion) to the high-rises of the CBD and the green hills stretching across the northern suburbs and as far

as the FNB Stadium (famed as Soccer City during the 2010 World Cup) on the edge of Soweto.

It was once part of a hotel and shopping complex that was among the city's most prestigious locations. The shopping center remains a hugely popular, if more middle class, shopping venue that is among the busiest in Johannesburg.

Yeoville Dinner Club
This tiny restaurant has only one table with 18 seats, but it serves the most expansive African menu in the city in a neighborhood that has attracted migrants from across the continent.

Yeoville isn't part of the artsy, hipster revival that has transformed other parts of Joburg. Its meals takes from what's fresh in the neighborhood market and pulls from all of the cultures and nations represented on the surrounding streets.

Small groups are seated together as if at a dinner party, and the menu changes constantly.

Yeoville Dinner Club, 24 Rockery St, Yeoville, Johannesburg; +27 (0)83 447 4235

Liliesleaf Farm
In 1963, police raided Liliesleaf Farm in Rivonia on the outskirts of Johannesburg and arrested leaders of the liberation movement.

That led to the Rivonia Trial where Nelson Mandela (who had been arrested earlier), Walter Sisulu, Govan Mbeki, Andrew Mlangeni, Raymond Mhlaba, Ahmed Kathrada, Elias Motsoaledi and Denis Goldberg were sentenced to life in prison.

Rivonia is now fully swept up in the city's suburban sprawl, but the farm reopened in 2008 as a museum that explains what life was like in the underground liberation movement.

Liliesleaf Farm, 7 George Ave, Rivonia, Johannesburg

Melville Koppies for hiking
In the middle of the city, the Melville Koppies stretch over 150 hectares with rocky outcropping (those are the koppies) covered with indigenous plants that produce delicate flowers in spring and rugged grasses in winter.

Hikers spend hours along the trails, within view of the city's skyscrapers. On Sundays, church groups gather for worship in flowing robes with singing and drums that rise over the rocks.

The park also holds an ancient furnace from the Iron Age, making it an unusual natural link from the ancient past to the urban present.

Arts on Main / Maboneng precinct
A decade ago, when a Sunday morning market opened in an old liquor warehouse, it was an

urban oasis surrounded by car repair shops, light industrial complexes, and derelict buildings.

But that modest start has grown into a massive urban renewal project that has lured top artists like William Kentridge, an art house cinema, young fashion designers and ambitious new chefs.

The neighborhoods new name, Maboneng, means "place of light." It's perhaps more accurately a place of exploring, as one of the few neighborhoods in Johannesburg that's easily traveled by foot along sidewalks that connect an ever-growing range of shops, restaurants and apartments.

Oriental Plaza

A shopping mall unlike any other in the city, Oriental Plaza hosts hundreds of stores that sell everything from spices to curtains to designer brands. It's on the edge of Fordsburg, the city's old

Indian neighborhood that now welcomes migrants from across the world.

The Plaza was built in the 1970s in an attempt to compensate Indian shop owners after the apartheid government razed a nearby community in its violent drive for racial separation.

The building stands rather oddly apart from the surrounding neighborhood, but has become a popular destination for people from across Johannesburg looking for fair prices and great Indian food.

Oriental Plaza, 38 Lilian Ngoyi St., Fordsburg, Johannesburg

Keyes Art Mile
A new collection of shops and restaurants link some of the city's finest art galleries in the Rosebank neighborhood: Everard Read and its new circular tower Circa, the Goodman Gallery, SMAC,

Southern Guild and Whatiftheworld. Upstairs is the exquisite new restaurant Marble.

Then there's the option of hamburgers and milkshakes at BGR on the ground floor and light lunches at the Milk Bar, which decorated by Amatulli importers with objects from across Africa.

Farther down the block at the corner of Jan Smuts Avenue and Bolton Road is a collection of hipster eateries, including the Bolton Collection, a barbershop bar, and a hidden speakeasy called Sin and Tax.

The galleries stay open late on the first Thursday of each month, becoming destinations for Johannesburg's beautiful people to see and be seen.

Keyes Art Mile, 19 Keyes Ave., Rosebank, Johannesburg

Soweto Derby
FNB City, the calabash-shaped stadium built for the 2010 World Cup, hosts the country's most epic soccer matches the Soweto Derby between the Kaizer Chiefs and the Orlando Pirates.

Loyalty to these crosstown Soweto rivals runs deep, but the atmosphere is celebratory.

For these matches, the stands overflow with music, dancing and costumes including makarapas, mining hats carved and painted into fantastic shapes.

Buy tickets early. There's little chance of finding one at the gate.

JoburgPlaces walking tour
The best way to experience Johannesburg's revival is with a walking tour by JoburgPlaces, led by Gerald Garner, who wrote a fascinating book of the same name.

He presents the stories of the city's past and present in a way that helps even locals appreciate how dramatically Johannesburg is changing from month to month.

Some tours run on specific themes, from the lighthearted rooftop bars tour to a six-hour walk throughout the inner city. The tours start and end at the new Joziburg Lane complex, an old car storage facility that's being turned into a foodie hub, market and loft apartments.

Have Dim Sum in the old Chinatown
More recent Chinese arrivals in Johannesburg have settled in a "new" Chinatown in Cyrildene, where streets are packed with Asian grocers, barbers and restaurants.

The original Chinatown was on the city's west end, and now offers a glimpse into the lives of the first Chinese migrants.

Historic markers along the sidewalks include photos and descriptions of the past, and neighborhood institutions like Sui Hing Hong grocery store and the Swallow's Inn are still going strong.

A relatively new arrival is Ming Woo at 4 Commissioner Street, which prepares steaming baskets of dim sum. The menu here is something of secret.

Diners who don't appear to be Chinese won't be offered the dim sum menu, but it's totally worth asking for.

Ratz Bar in Melville
Melville attracts a mix of students, artists, and people who like being around them. Like the rest of Johannesburg, the neighborhood has gone through a series of changes that leave it

sometimes feeling a bit more empty, sometimes a bit overcrowded.

Right now Melville is back at a high point, with cafes, bookstores and quirky boutiques pulling in a mixed clientele. There's always been a gay scene along 7th Street, and Ratz Bar is one of the mainstays that has endured through the street's ups and downs.

It's friendly, heavy on 80s music, with good bar food. And it's a great jumping off point for exploring the rest of the neighborhood.

Ratz Bar Melville, 9 7th St., Melville, Johannesburg; +27 (0)11 482 2414

Emirates Airline Park
Still popularly known as Ellis Park, this stadium hosted the 1995 rugby World Cup final, when Nelson Mandela donned the Springbok jersey to present the South African team the trophy in what

became a symbol of reconciliation after the fall of apartheid. The events were also the inspiration for the 2009 film "Invictus" starring Morgan Freeman.

For visitors, first prize is of course to attend a match, but the stadium also has a museum with a staggering collection of Springbok memorabilia that's on display weekdays.

Northern Farm
Northern Farm opens its 1,600 hectares to the public on weekends and holidays for cycling, horse riding, hiking and picnics.

Some areas of the farm are actual farmland, but others are open grasslands, clusters of trees, and small reservoirs filled by rivers and canals. Even though it's close to the city and popular with cyclists, Northern Farm remains relatively unknown to travelers, but is perfect for a quick and quiet getaway from town.

Johannesburg, South Africa

Northern Farm Nature Reserve, R114 & Falkirk Road, Diepsloot

City Central Food Hall
Once the lavish headquarters of Barclays Bank in South Africa,, the building at 85 Commissioner Street, which was empty for years, has reopened as the City Central Food Hall, where vendors prepare innovative meals on weekdays for breakfast and lunch.

Generous portions of smoked meats, gourmet burgers, dim sum, and curries are served up under an enormous skylight in the triple-volume banking hall. Upstairs on the mezzanine, the Brass Bar serves drinks on the balcony and Bridge Books keeps coffee and a collection of African literature by the roof deck.

City Central Food Hall, 85 Commissioner St., Johannesburg

Nirox Sculpture Park
The lush grounds of the Nirox Sculpture Park are only open for exhibitions and events, but it's so beautiful that it's worth planning around them for a visit there.

Guests are invited to wander the grounds of what was a trout farm.

Although the Nirox Foundation hosts artist residencies, it's best known for its annual sculpture fair and its series of outdoor concerts.

Nirox Sculpture Park, 24 Kromdraai Rd, Kromdraai, Krugersdorp; +27 82 854 6963

The Grind Coffee Company
This coffee shop inside a bike shop serves espresso in an ice cream cone.

This coffee shop inside a bike shop asks customers if they want a cup or a cone, but it's espresso, not ice cream, that's on offer.

They line the inside of ice cream cones with a thick layer of chocolate, then carefully pour the coffee into it. The hot drink melts the chocolate into a sweet drink that tastes delicious, but isn't meant to linger over.

Drink the coffee before all the chocolate melts, or the cone will go soggy and start to leak.

The Grind Coffee Company, 34 Whiteley Road, Melrose Arch, Johannesburg; +27 (0) 72 754 8705

Gandhi House
A century ago, Mahatma Gandhi lived in Johannesburg, where his encounters with racism helped inspire his philosophy of passive resistance, or Satyagraha.

His one-time lodgings are now a guest house and museum known as Satyagraha House, where visitors can go on a tour or sleep in one of seven rooms of the home designed by architect Hermann Kallenbach for Gandhi and himself.

It recently underwent a simple but gorgeous restoration, and offers yoga and meditation in the garden, with vegetarian meals for overnight guests.

Satyagraha House, 15 Pine Road & Garden Road, Orchard, Johannesburg

Fashion District

Johannesburg's historic garment district has become revitalized with a more traditionally African design sense. The Fashion District store (109 Pritchard Street) supplies tailors and designers, whose work is on display in the surrounding streets.

Next door, Studio 109 has a staggering selection of traditional shweshwe prints, which get used as modern finishes in shops like Urban Zulu, which began nearby but has opened branches across the city.

Origins Center
Top South African artists created the displays for this museum which interprets the fossil findings that have cast light on the earliest evolution of humanity found just outside the city.

The museum is interactive in a way geared more towards adults, and explores the beliefs and culture of the region's earliest inhabitants, the San Bushmen.

Origins Center, Yale Road & Enoch Sontonga Avenue, Johannesburg

Maropeng in the Cradle of Humankind
The remains of some of humanity's earliest ancestors were discovered on the outskirts of Johannesburg, in a region now preserved as the Cradle of Humankind.

Maropeng visitor's center explains evolution from the first life on Earth to modern humans, taking care to deconstruct the racist notions that once denied Africa's role as the birthplace of humanity.

The buildings were designed to blend into the landscape. Nearby caves hold active dig sites, some also open to visitors.

Maropeng, just off the R563 Hekpoort Road, Sterkfontein; +27 (0)14 577 9000

The Orbit jazz club
A landmark on Johannesburg's music scene, the Orbit showcases the best in jazz from South Africa and around the region.

The club hosts poetry nights, and periodic cocktails with scientists, for intimate discussions with South Africa's brightest minds.

The Orbit, 81 De Korte St, Bramfontein, Johannesburg; +27 (0)11 339 6645

Take a trip to Lion Park

The wildlife conservation known as Lion Park is dedicated to the protection of Transvaal lions and is spread over 500 acres of land in the Gauteng province. More than 80 lions live in the park (including some rare white lions), along with many other carnivores such as cheetahs, Cape wild dogs, spotted hyenas, black-backed jackal and a wide range of antelopes. Don't miss the rare opportunity to see such splendid wildlife variety that has even attracted famous celebrities. An outing like this is perfect for the entire family.

Visit Croc City Crocodile & Reptile Park

How many opportunities will you get to see a crocodile farm? Situated in close proximity to the Lion Park, Croc City Crocodile & Reptile Park is one of the world's favorite wildlife filming venues for crocodiles and other reptiles. The park provides a great experience for the whole family. Don't miss feeding time as the crocodiles wrestle each other for chickens. Best of all, you can have a photo taken holding a baby crocodile or a snake. Be sure to check out the snake show, and once you've seen everything the park has to offer you can go for a meal at the pizza restaurant

See the Golden Rhinoceros of Mapungubwe
The ruins of Mapungubwe were discovered in 1932. They provide evidence not only of the early smiting of gold in southern Africa, but also of the extravagant wealth and social differentiation of the people of Mapungubwe. Among the ruins a gold foil rhinoceros was found molded over a soft core of sculpted wood. A replica of the gold rhinoceros was erected on Fox Street, just opposite the Hollard Street pedestrian mall. The Limpopo province, where the discovery was made, has been designated a UNESCO World Heritage Site. Many people stop by The Golden Rhinoceros

of Mapungubwe to take a photo with this historical gem.

Have a grand time at Gold Reef City

Gold Reef City is an amusement park located on a gold mine that was closed in 1971. Come and enjoy a wide variety of fun rides be aware that some have height restrictions. Here, visitors also get the opportunity to learn about real life mining disasters. For an additional fee, you can take part in an underground tour of a disused gold mine. One ride to look forward to is the giant wheel, which provides a stunning view of Johannesburg's suburbs and the beautiful calabash of Soccer City. Test out your luck at the casino afterwards.

Place your bet at Montecasino

If you find yourself in the Sandton area you could make a trip to Montecasino. The leisure and casino complex covers 26 hectares of land and there are buskers and street performers wandering around entertaining visitors. Montecasino was first opened in November 30, 2000. It presently attracts 9.3 million visitors annually who are amazed by the theatrics and high-quality entertainment. The main casino building boasts a fake sky painted on the roof that goes from light to dark from one side to the other.

Spend a Day at Lesedi Cultural Village

A visit to Lesedi Cultural Village is always fulfilling, as the place allows visitors to get a glimpse of the different South African tribes and cultures. Located near the Hartbeespoort Dam, the Lesedi Cultural Village reproduces traditional houses and offers demonstrations of dances and other traditions of the Zulu, Xhosa, Pedi, Basotho, Nguni and Ndebele people. For a reasonable price you get to sleep in colorfully decorated traditional huts equipped with bathrooms. You can also sample authentic African cuisines prepared by talented local cooks.

Dine and shop at Fresh Earth Food Store
Located on Komatie Street, Fresh Earth Food Store was established with the aim of fostering a new understanding of healthy eating and sustainability. Its delicious vegetarian dishes are prepared from scratch and they don't contain any artificial additives, sweeteners, colorants or preservatives, so the meals are nutritious and healthy. Not only does Fresh Earth offer tasty vegetarian treats, but here you can also shop for healthy groceries, supplements and baby food. It also stocks cleaning products and kitchen equipment. One added bonus are the detailed vegetarian recipes available for free at the store.

Caleb Gray

The End

www.ingramcontent.com/pod-product-compliance
Lightning Source LLC
Chambersburg PA
CBHW031108080526
44587CB00011B/882